# Edgar Allen Poe
# An Adult Coloring Book

## By Peaceful Mind Adult Coloring Books

Copyright © 2017

All rights reserved. No part of this publication may be reproduced, distributed, or transmitted in any form or by any means, including photocopying, recording, or other electronic or mechanical methods, without the prior written permission of the publisher

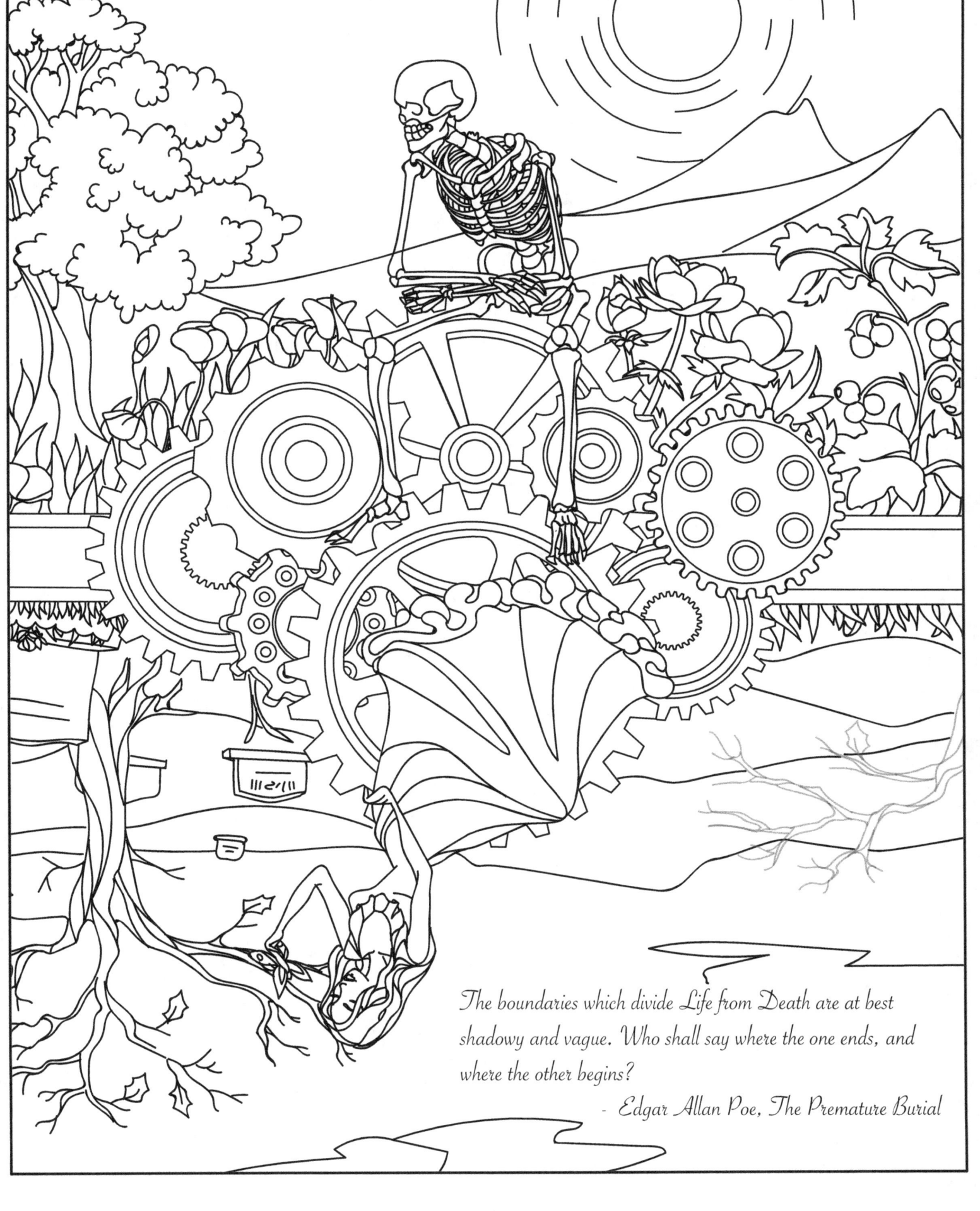

*The boundaries which divide Life from Death are at best shadowy and vague. Who shall say where the one ends, and where the other begins?*

— Edgar Allan Poe, The Premature Burial

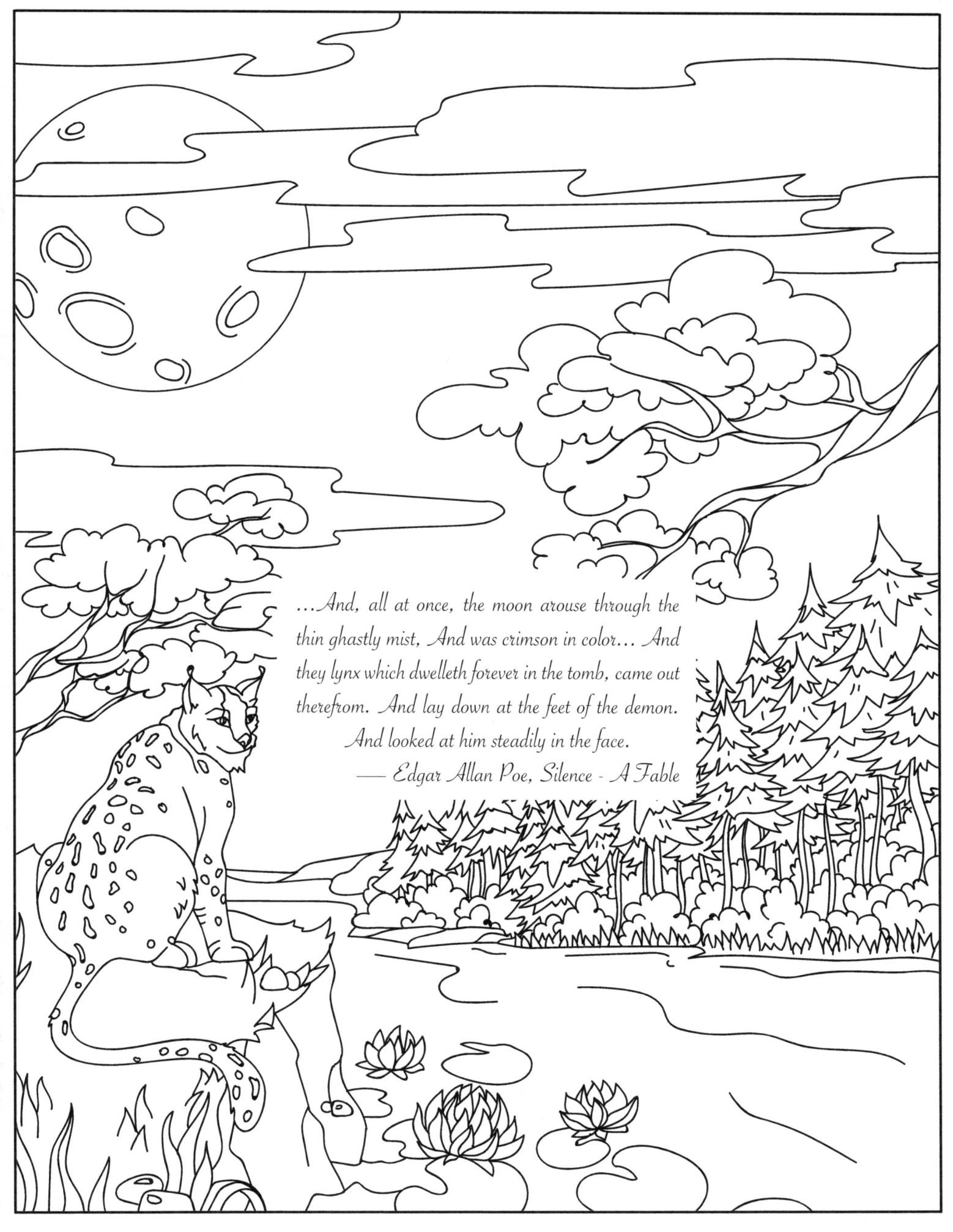

…And, all at once, the moon arouse through the thin ghastly mist, And was crimson in color… And they lynx which dwelleth forever in the tomb, came out therefrom. And lay down at the feet of the demon. And looked at him steadily in the face.
—— Edgar Allan Poe, Silence - A Fable

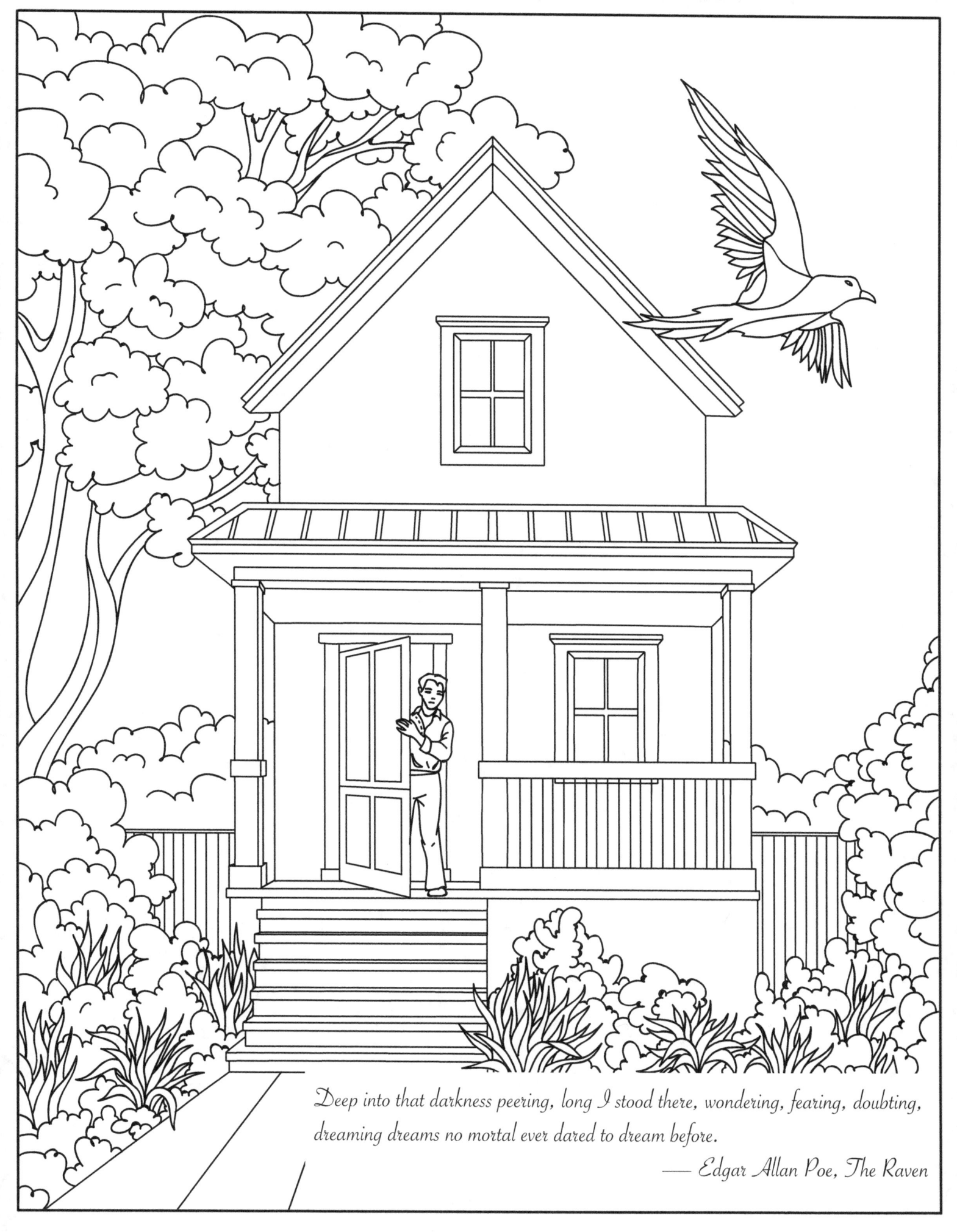

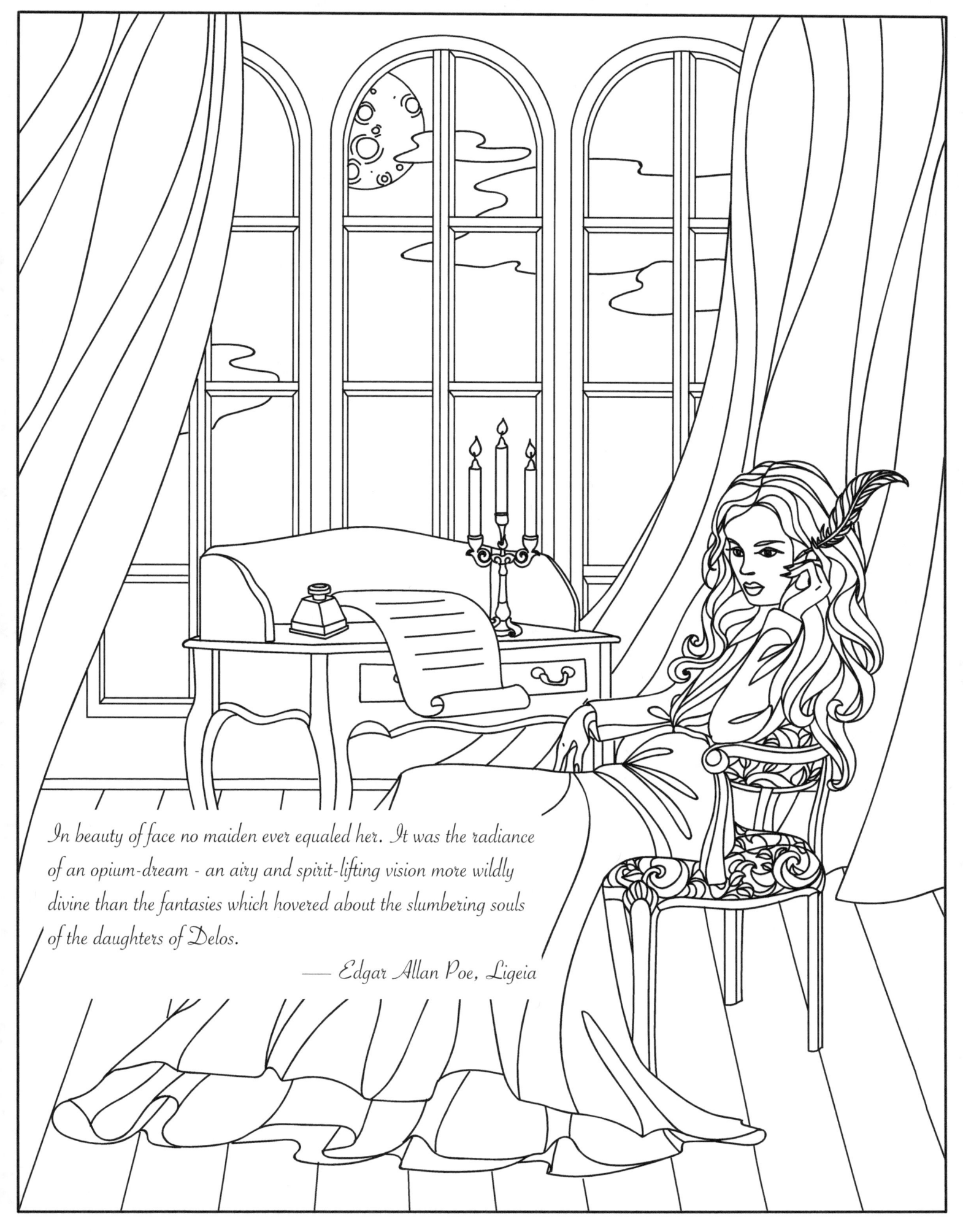

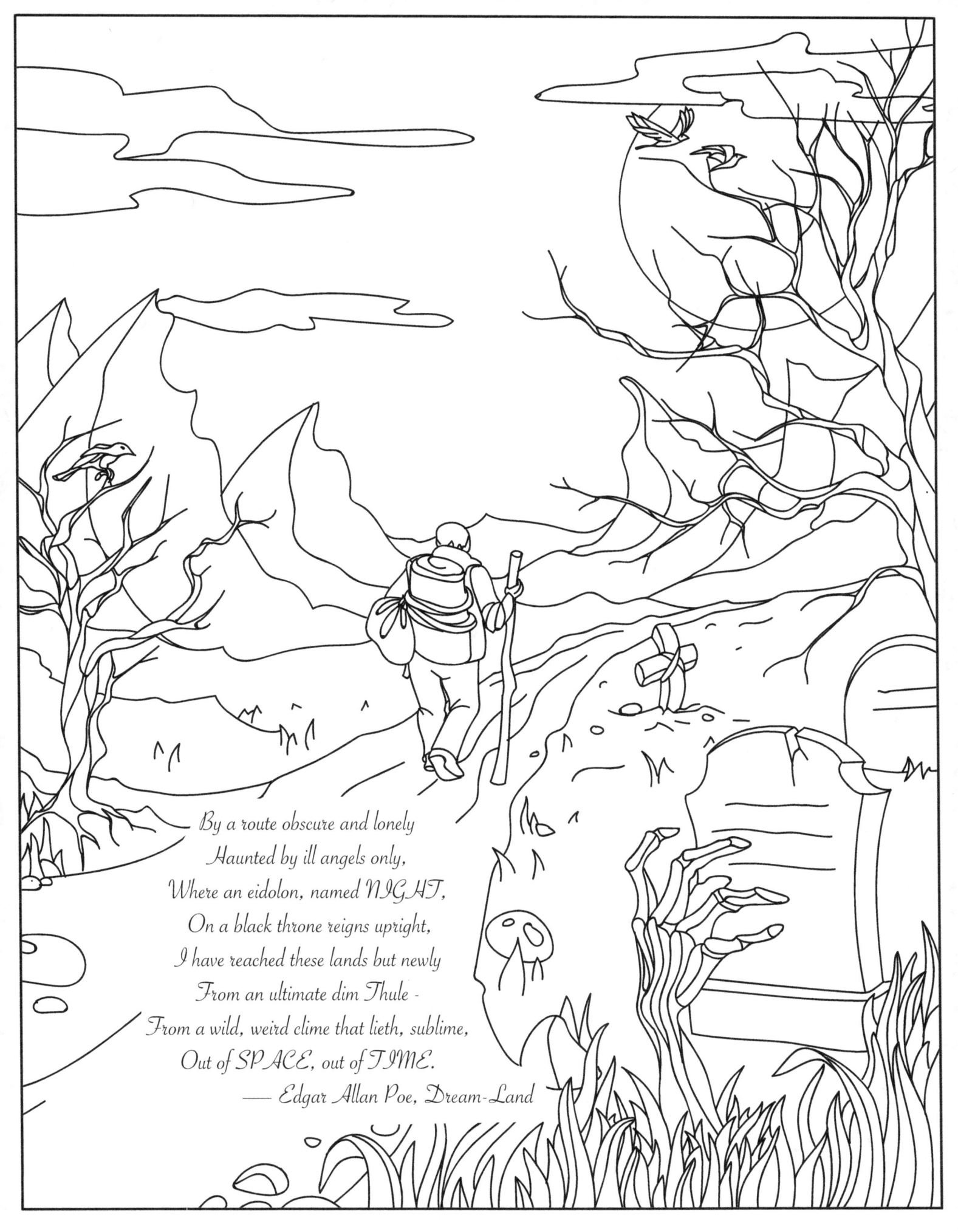

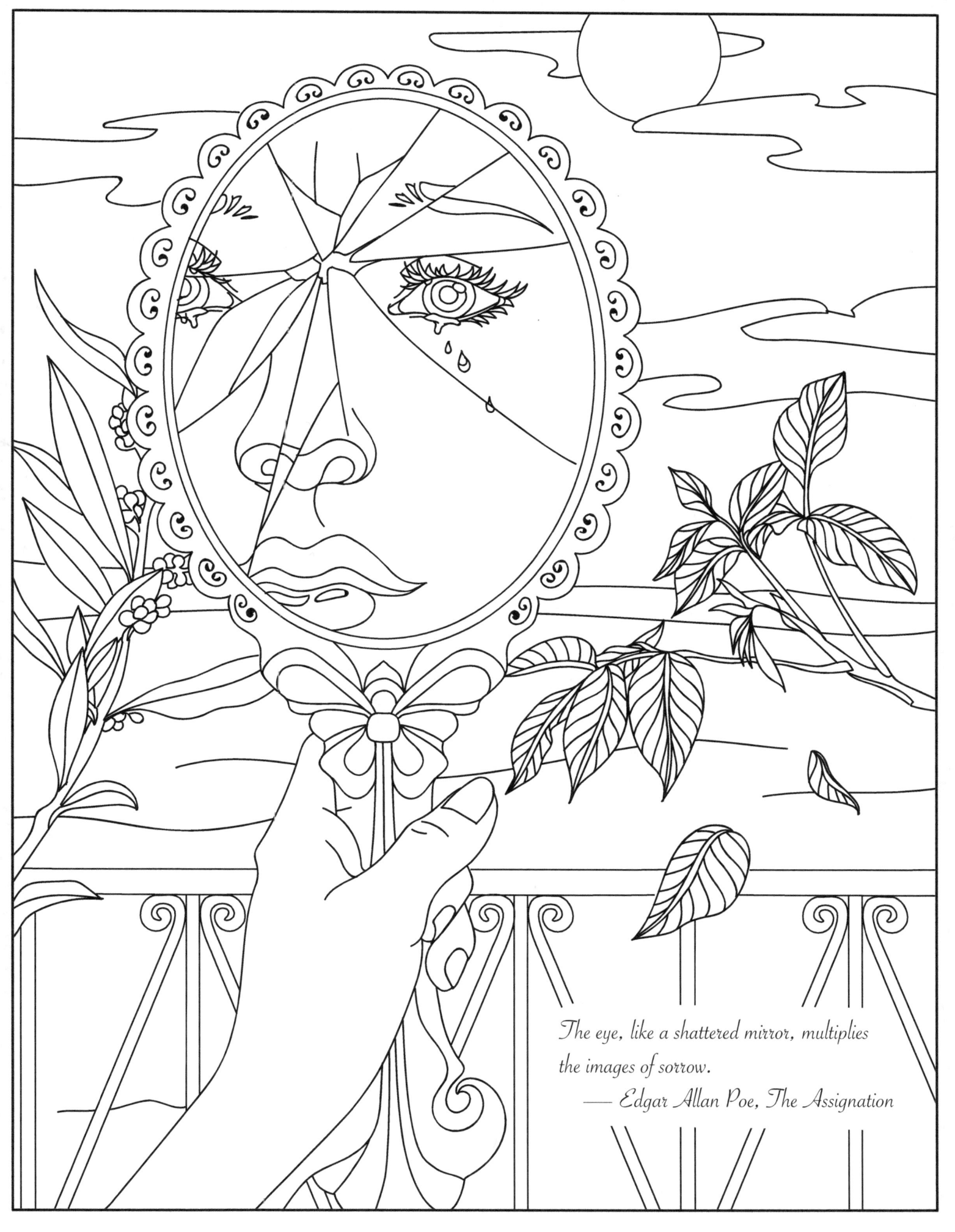

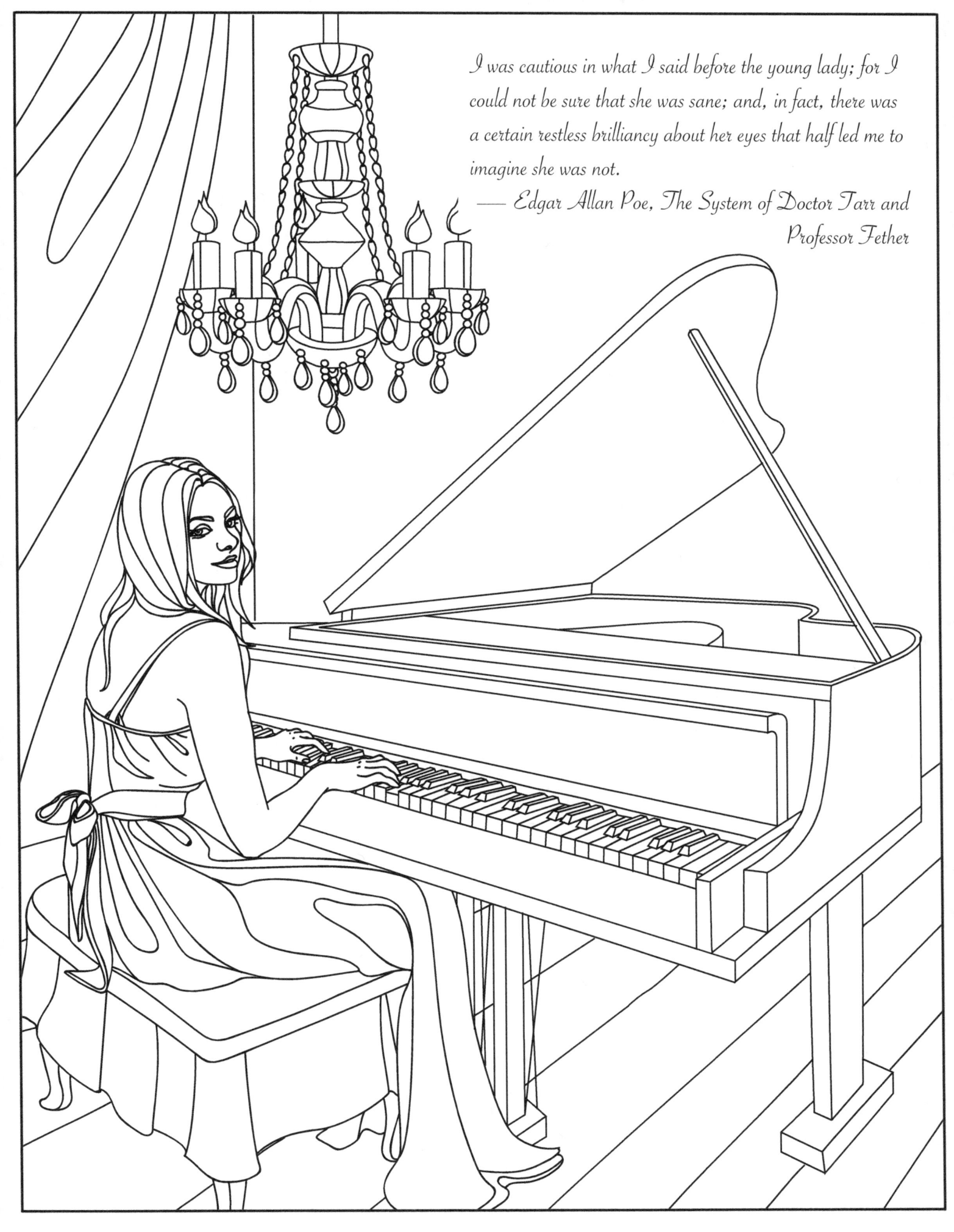

*I was cautious in what I said before the young lady; for I could not be sure that she was sane; and, in fact, there was a certain restless brilliancy about her eyes that half led me to imagine she was not.*
— Edgar Allan Poe, *The System of Doctor Tarr and Professor Fether*

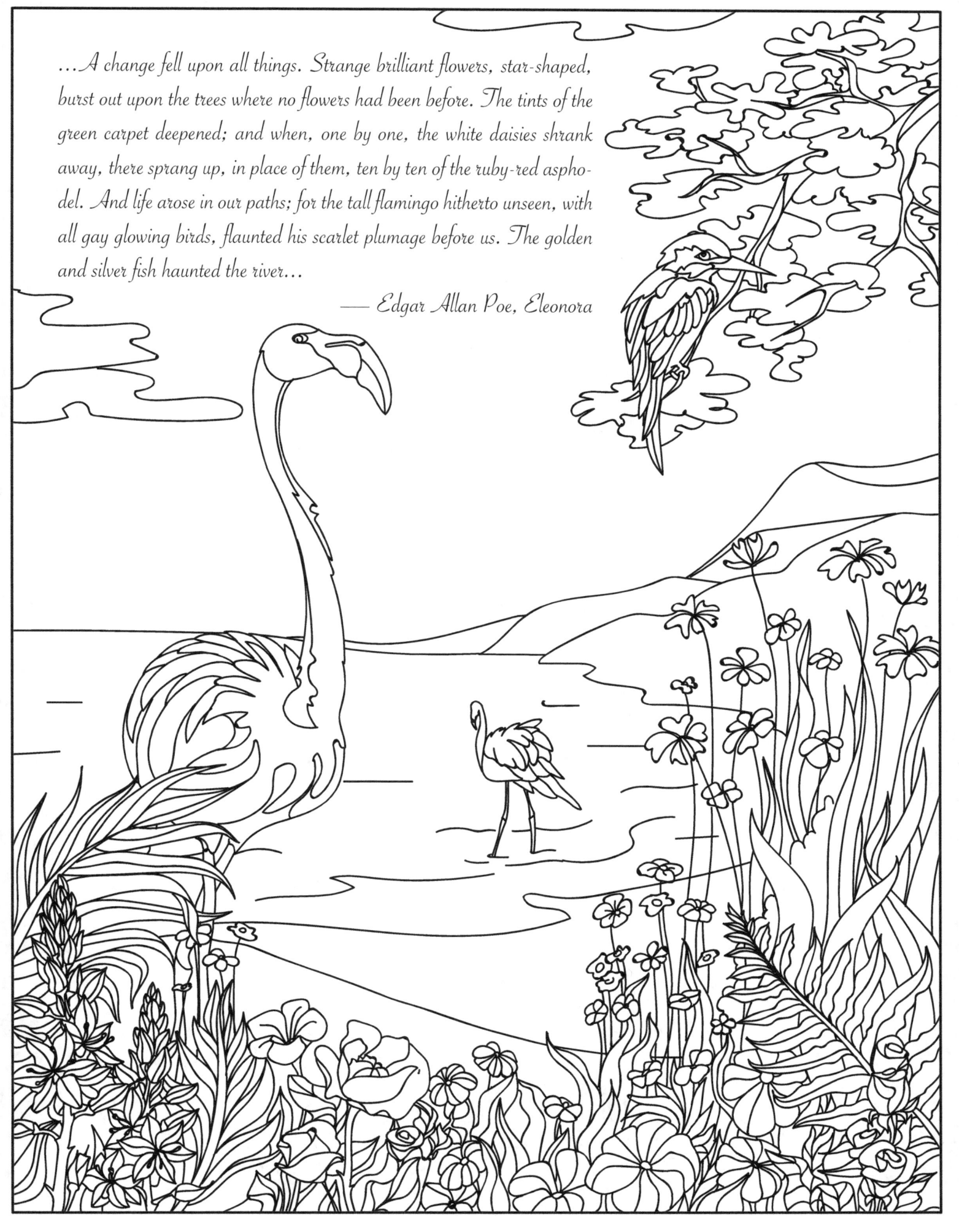

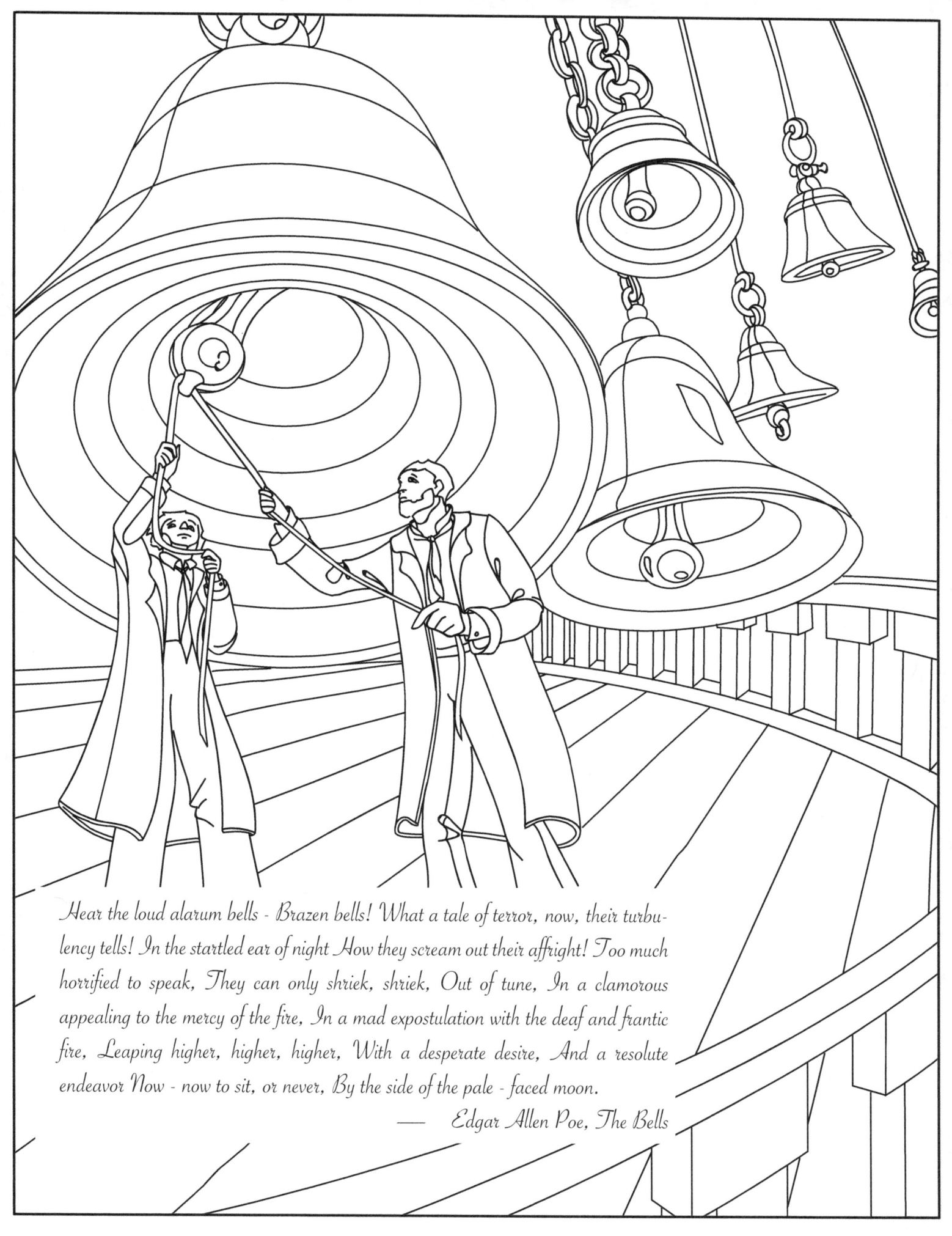

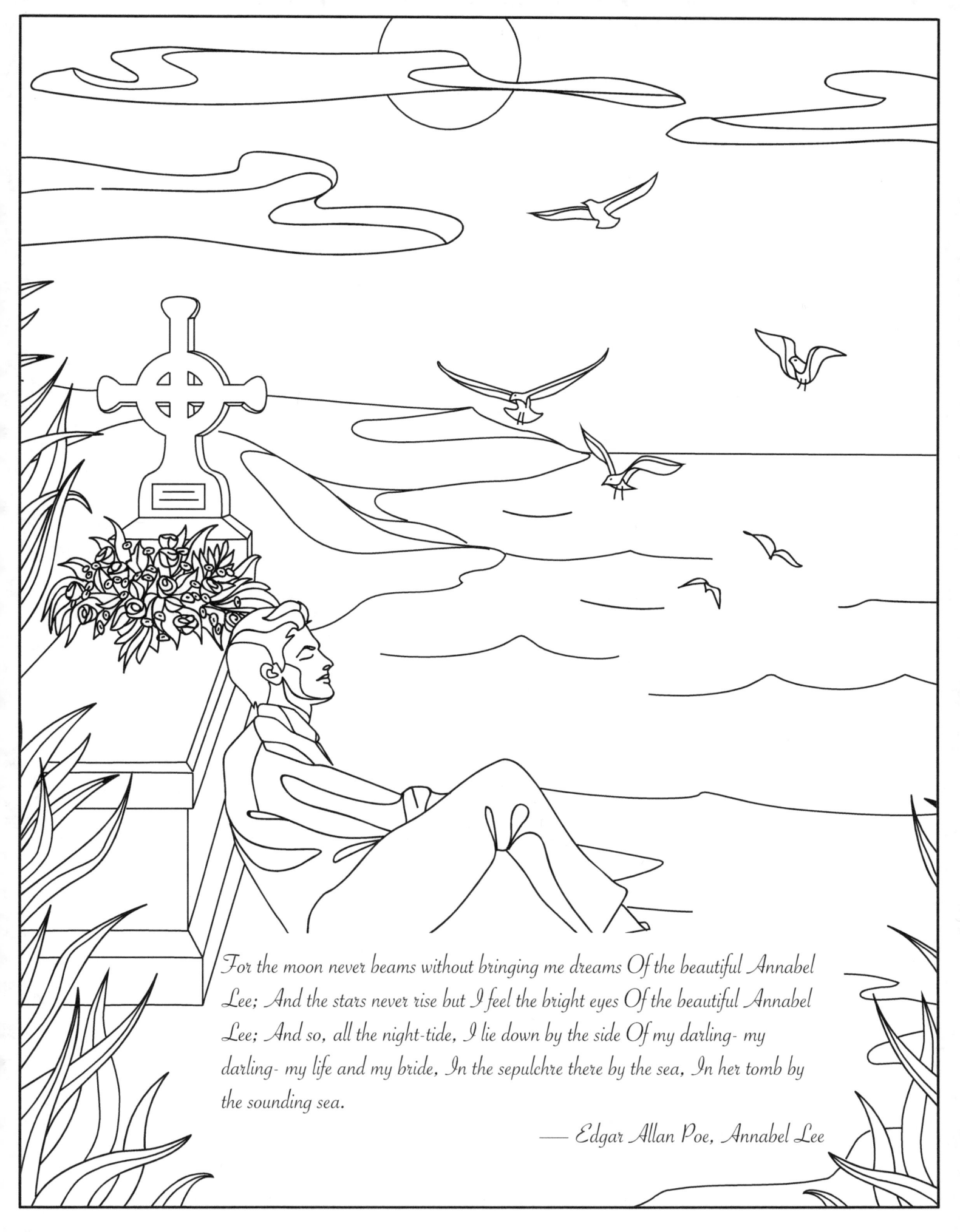

*For the moon never beams without bringing me dreams Of the beautiful Annabel Lee; And the stars never rise but I feel the bright eyes Of the beautiful Annabel Lee; And so, all the night-tide, I lie down by the side Of my darling- my darling- my life and my bride, In the sepulchre there by the sea, In her tomb by the sounding sea.*

— *Edgar Allan Poe, Annabel Lee*

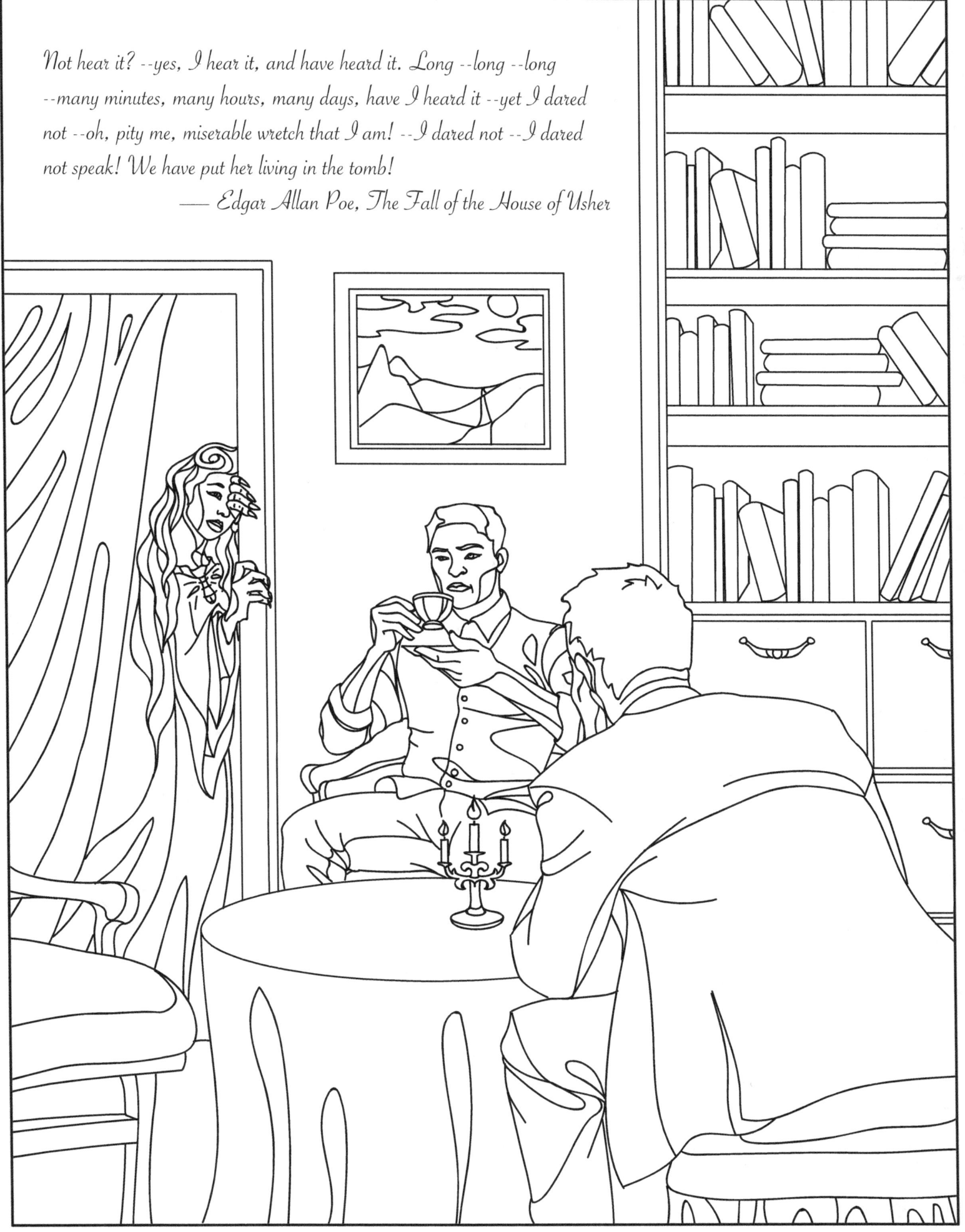

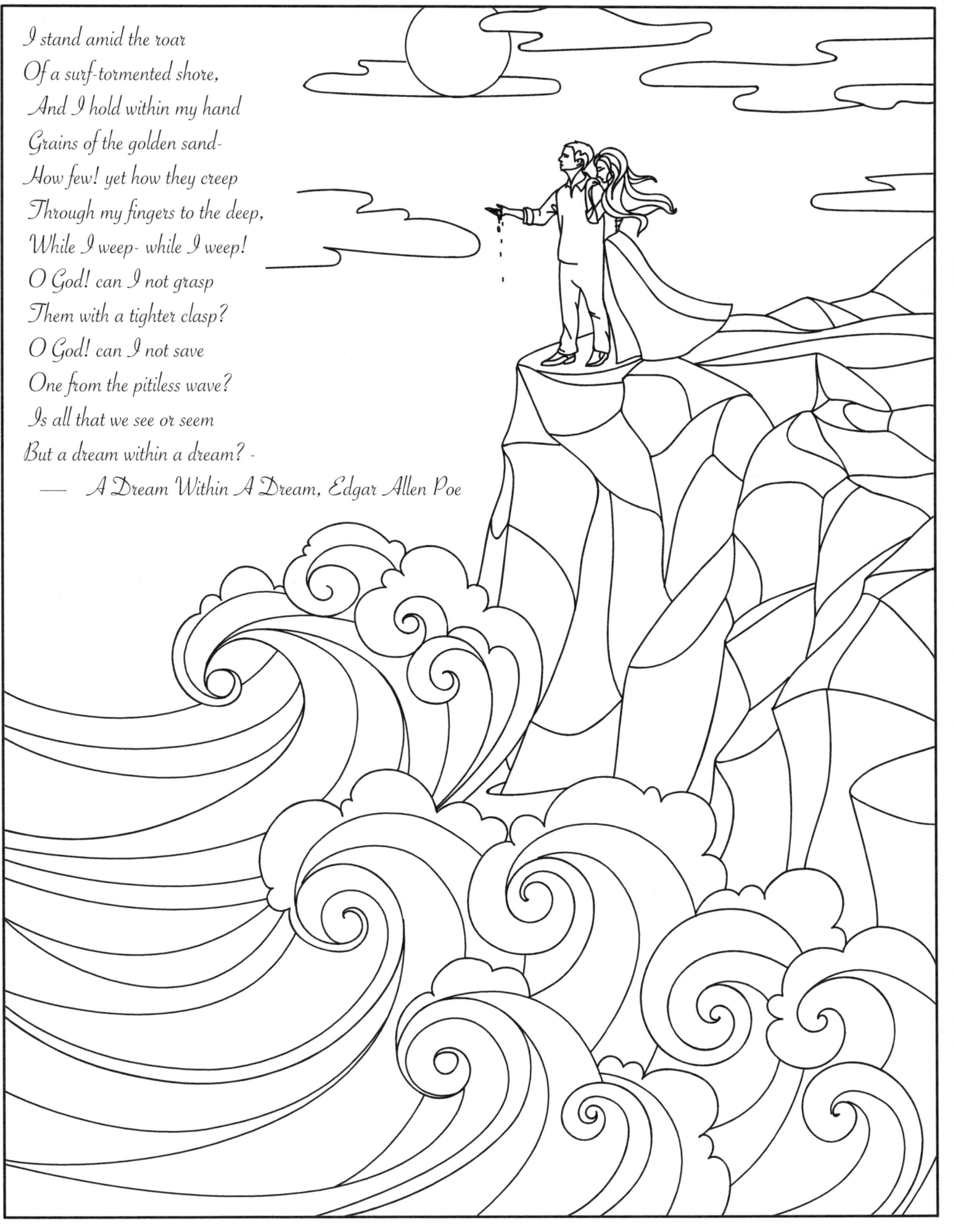

*I stand amid the roar*
*Of a surf-tormented shore,*
*And I hold within my hand*
*Grains of the golden sand-*
*How few! yet how they creep*
*Through my fingers to the deep,*
*While I weep- while I weep!*
*O God! can I not grasp*
*Them with a tighter clasp?*
*O God! can I not save*
*One from the pitiless wave?*
*Is all that we see or seem*
*But a dream within a dream? -*
— *A Dream Within A Dream, Edgar Allen Poe*

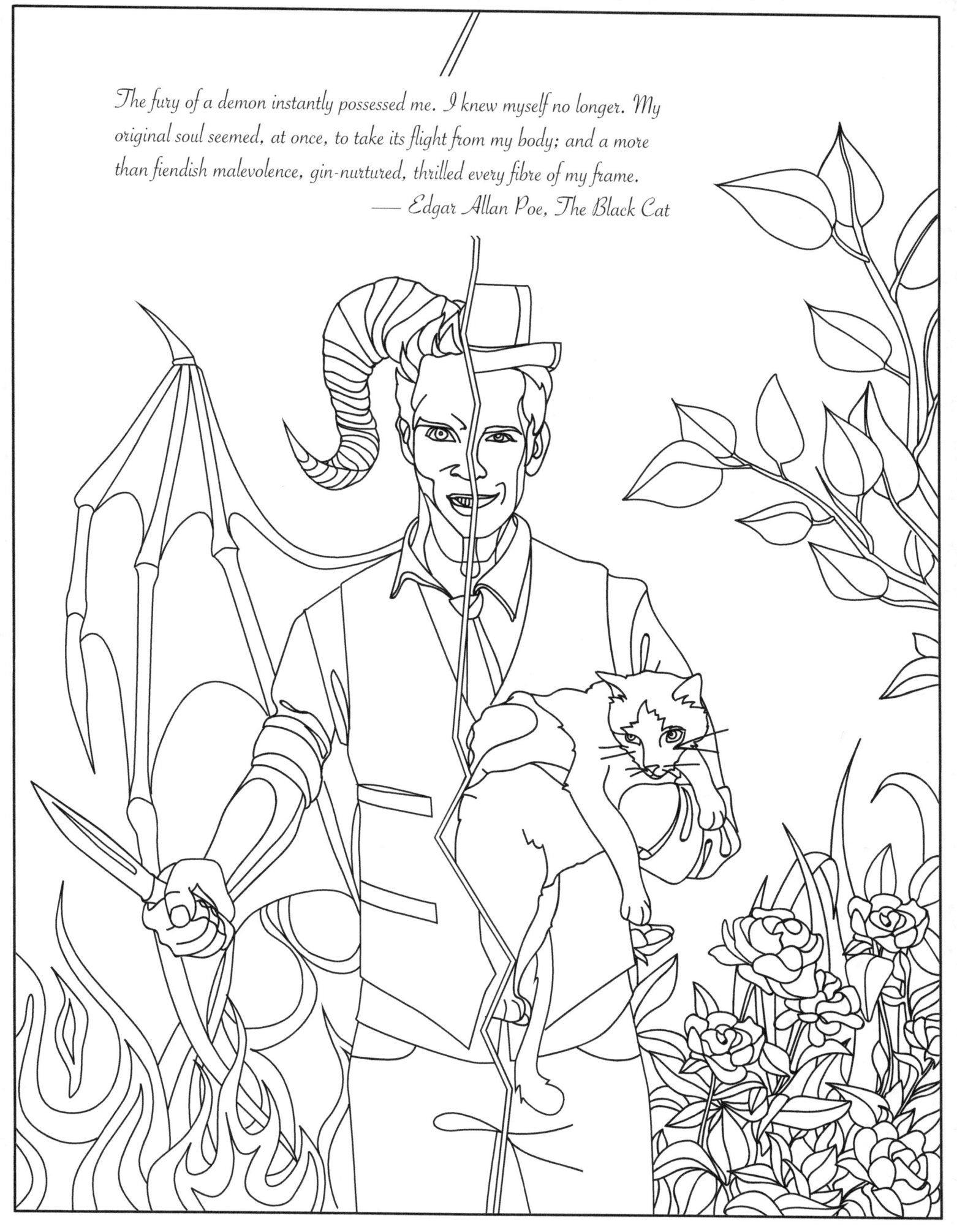

*The fury of a demon instantly possessed me. I knew myself no longer. My original soul seemed, at once, to take its flight from my body; and a more than fiendish malevolence, gin-nurtured, thrilled every fibre of my frame.*
— *Edgar Allan Poe, The Black Cat*

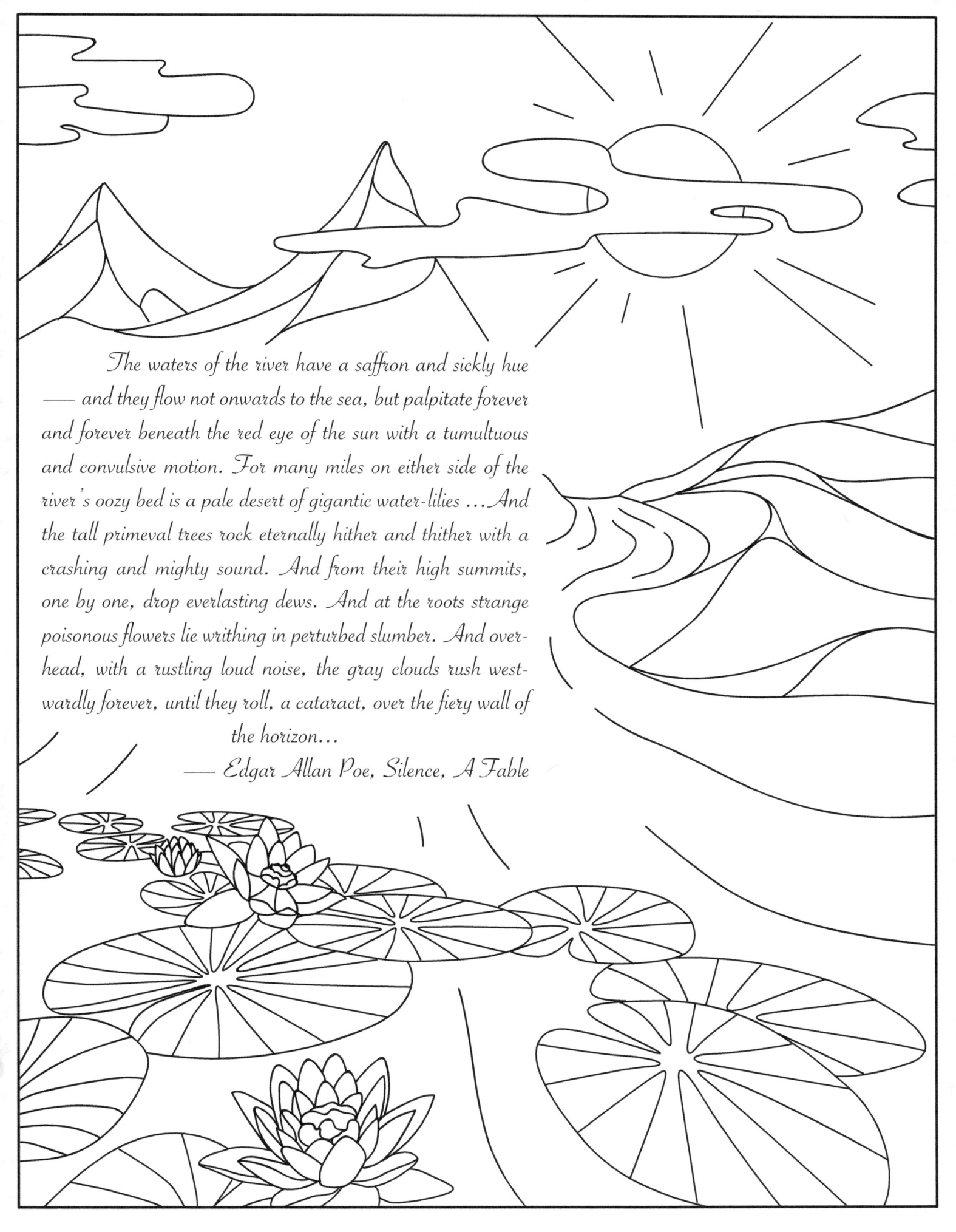

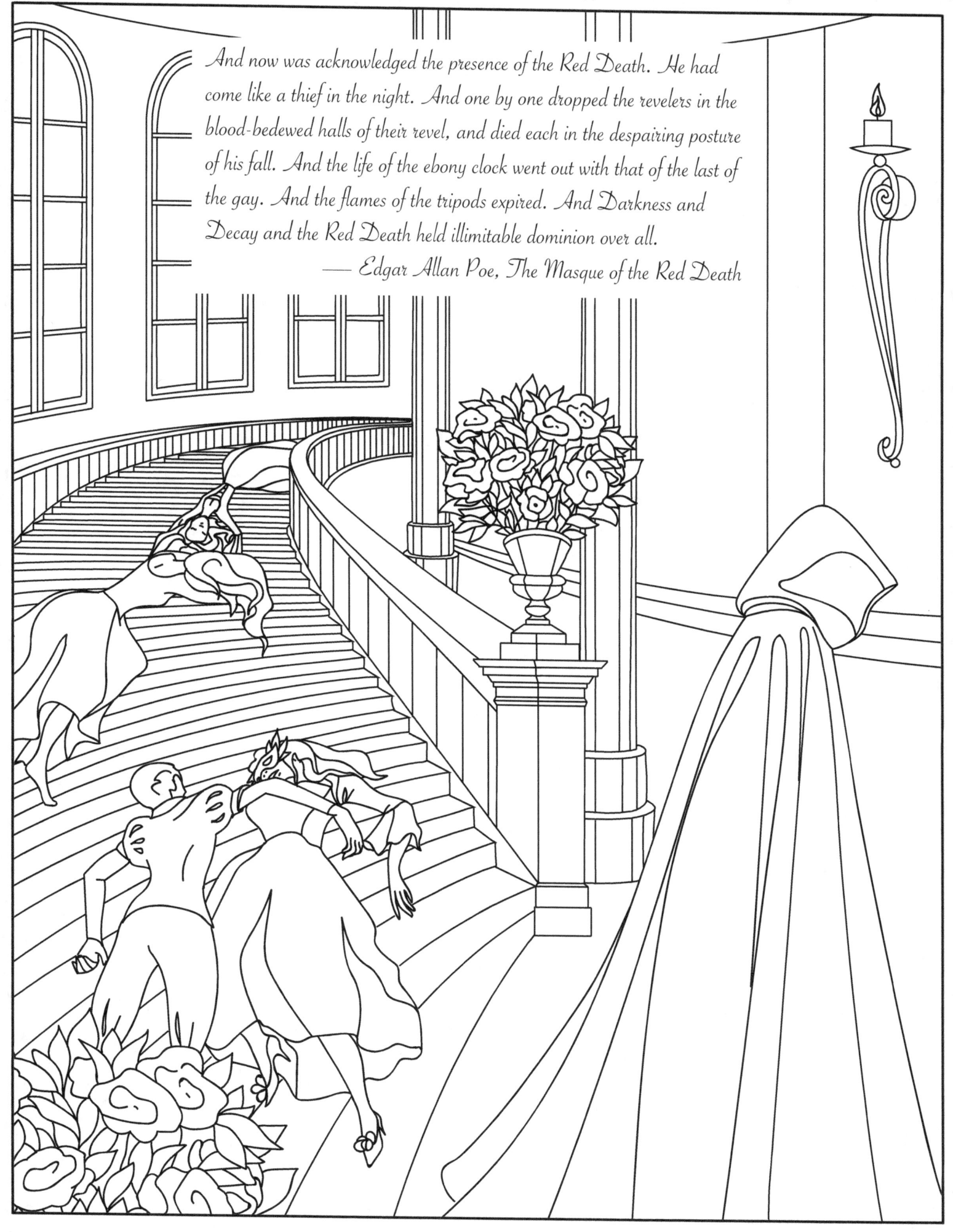

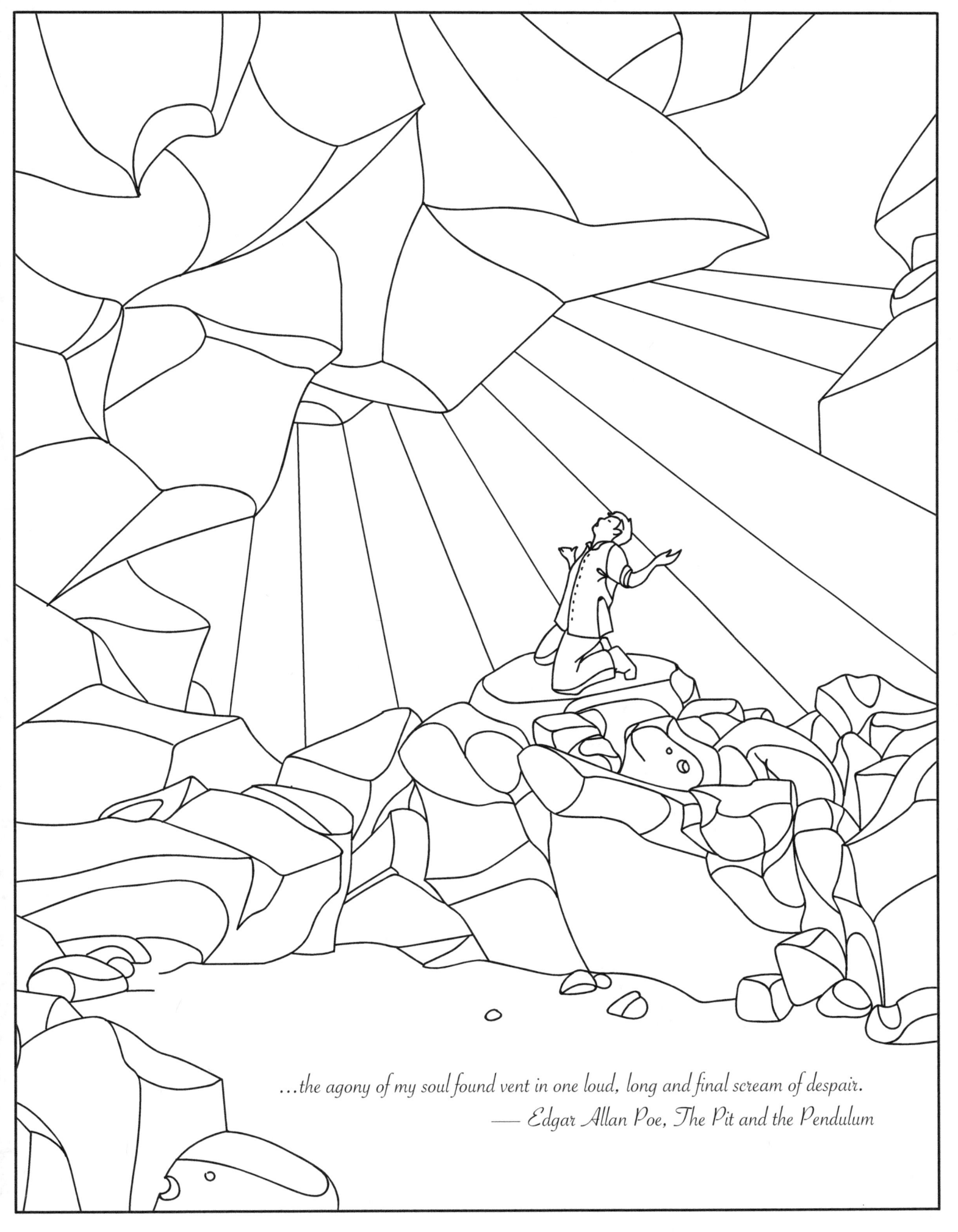

...the agony of my soul found vent in one loud, long and final scream of despair.
— Edgar Allan Poe, The Pit and the Pendulum

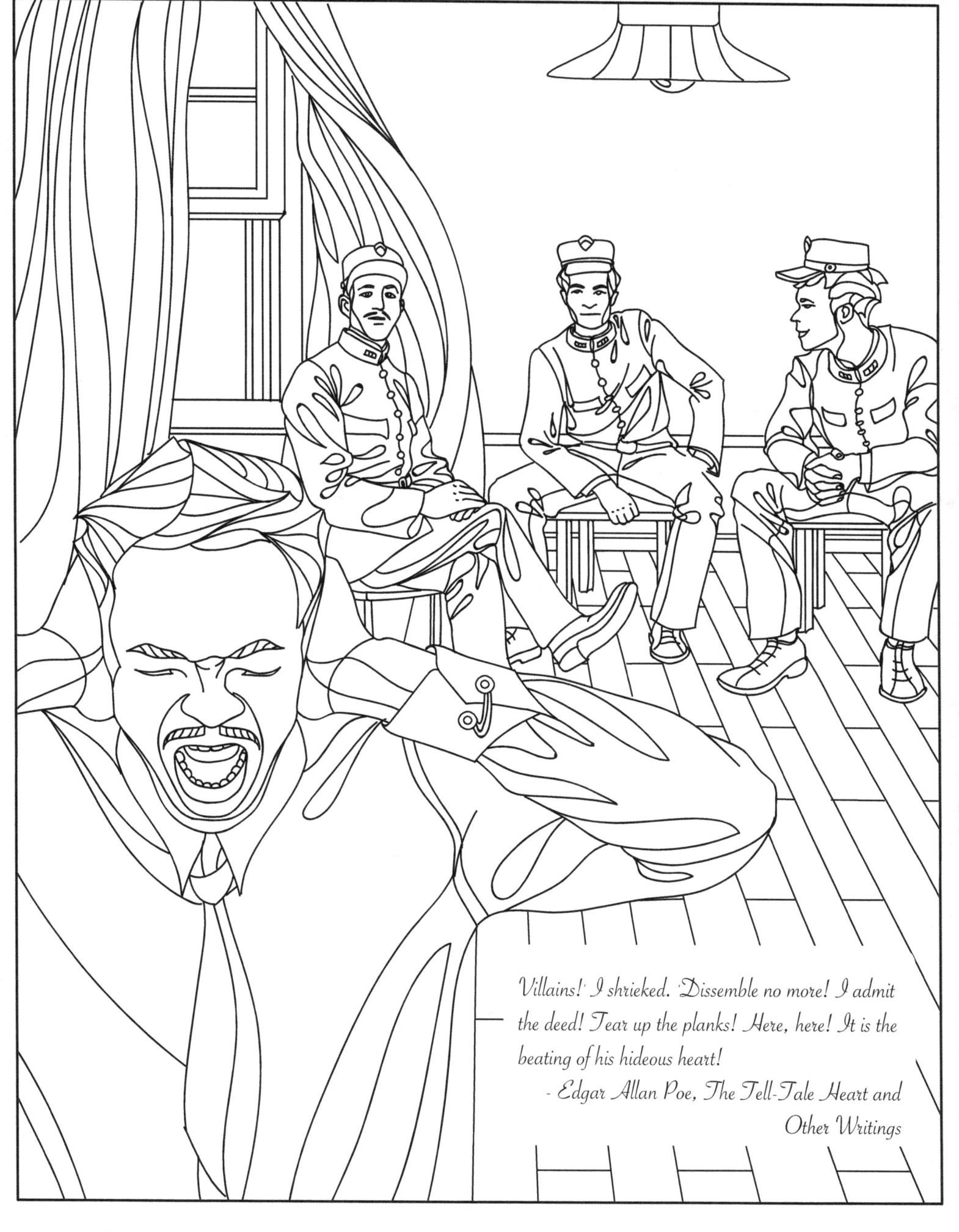

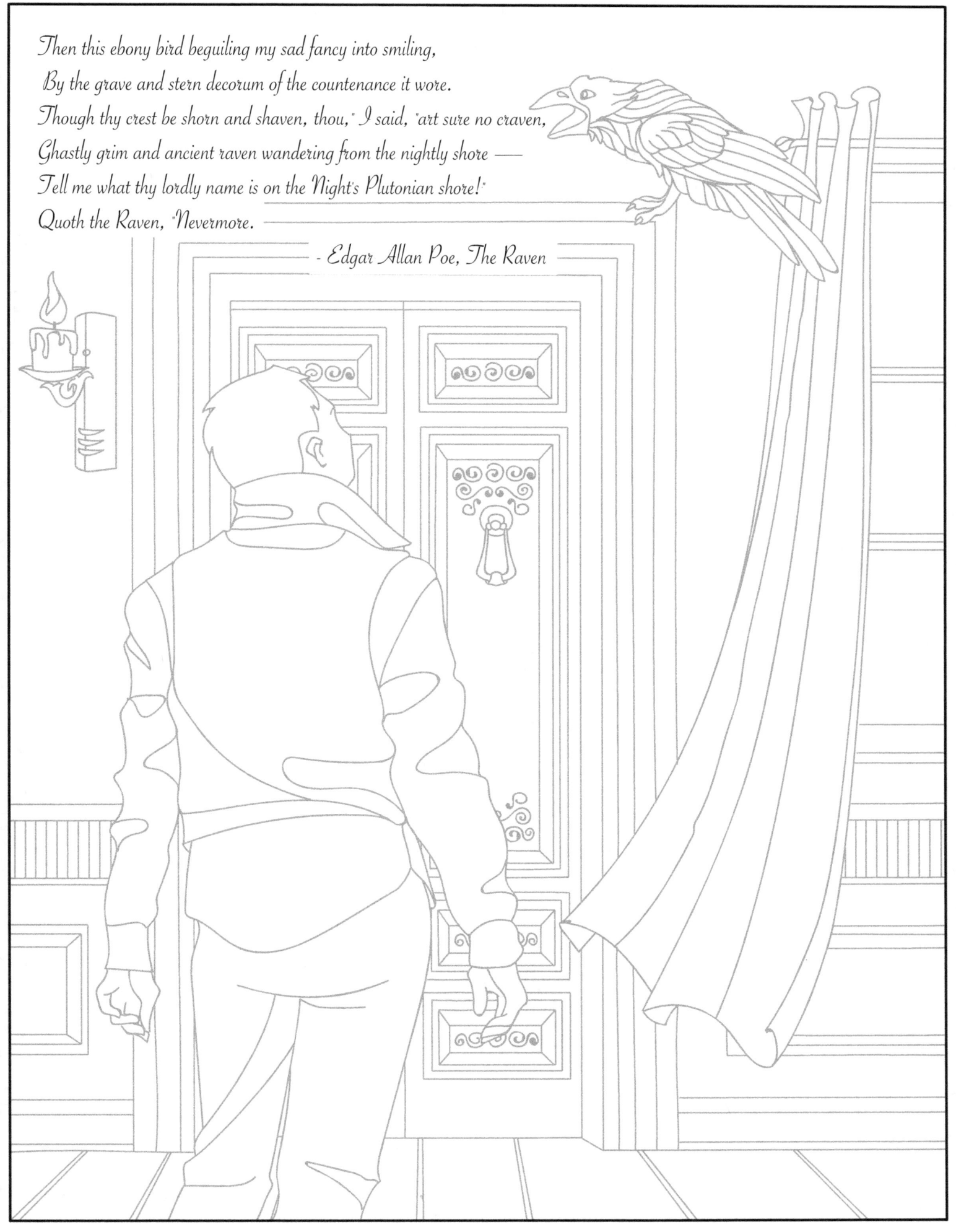

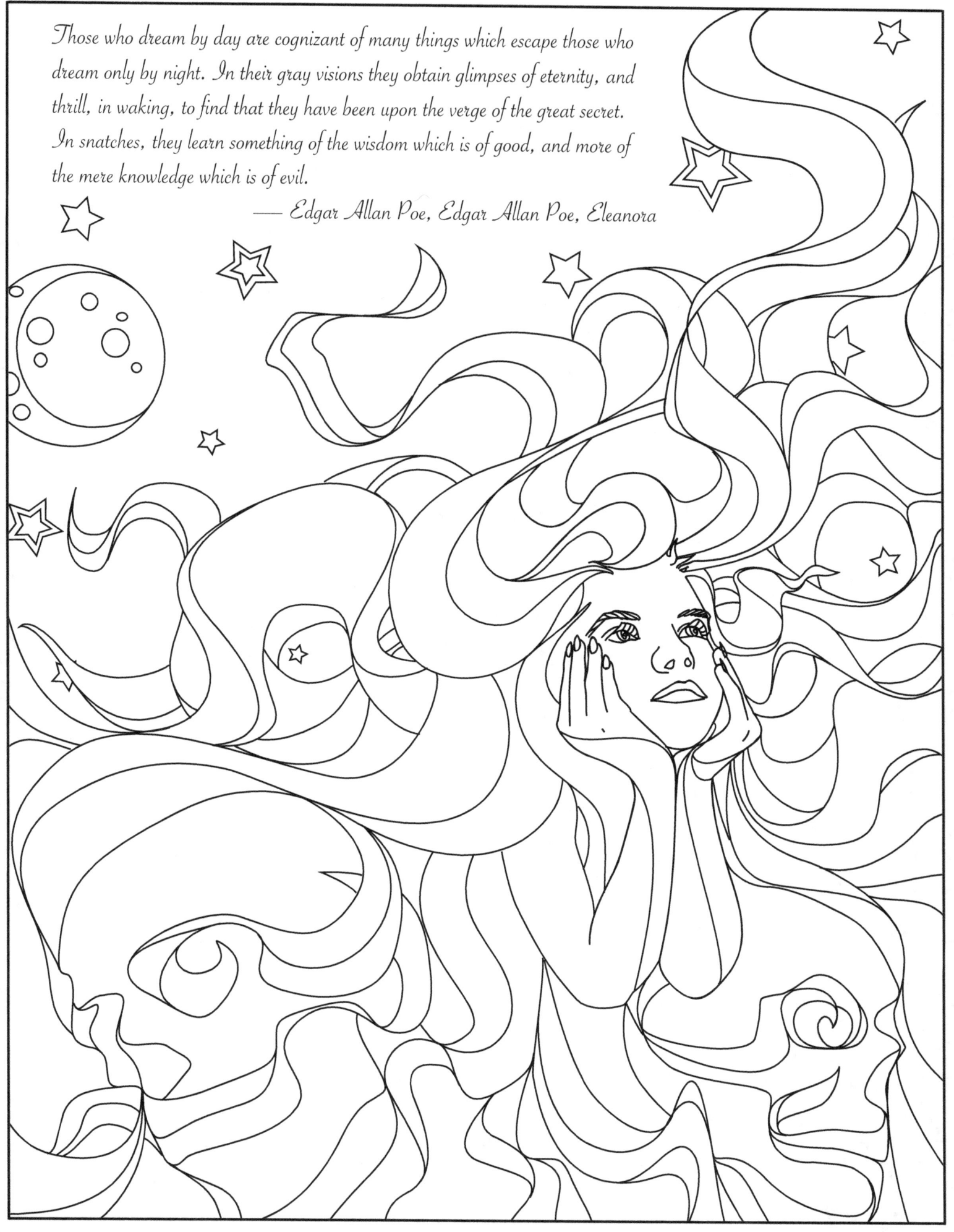

*Those who dream by day are cognizant of many things which escape those who dream only by night. In their gray visions they obtain glimpses of eternity, and thrill, in waking, to find that they have been upon the verge of the great secret. In snatches, they learn something of the wisdom which is of good, and more of the mere knowledge which is of evil.*
— *Edgar Allan Poe, Edgar Allan Poe, Eleanora*

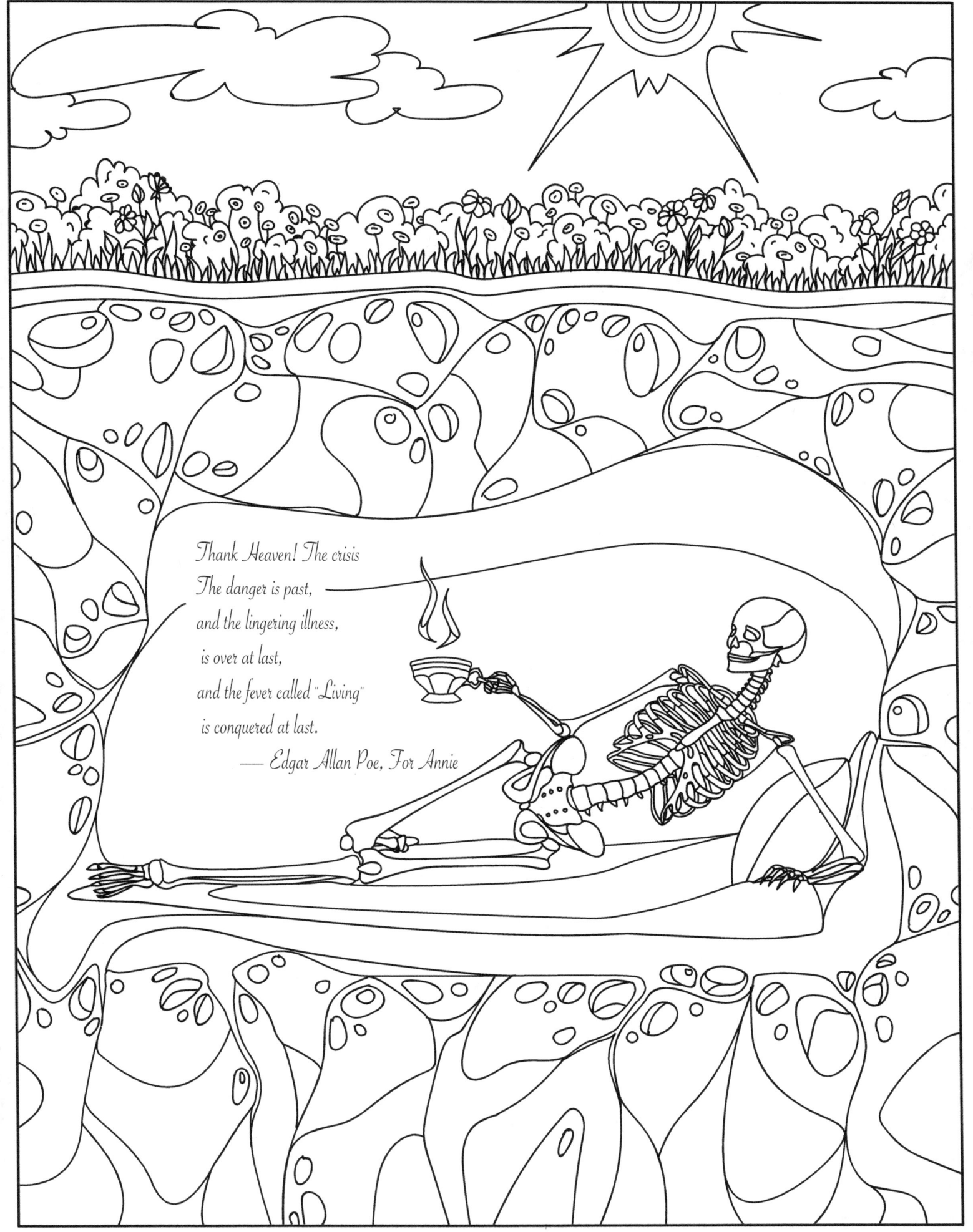

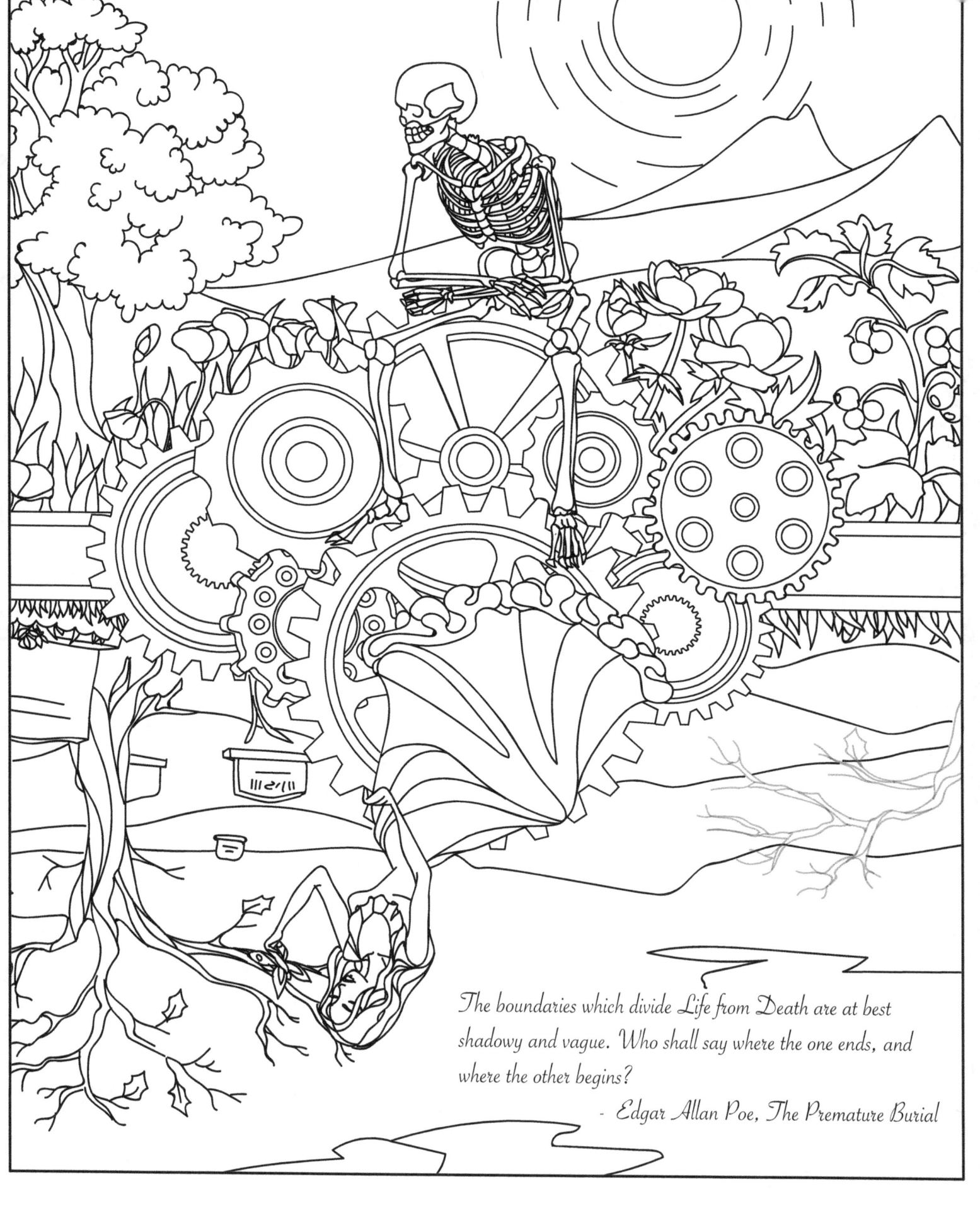

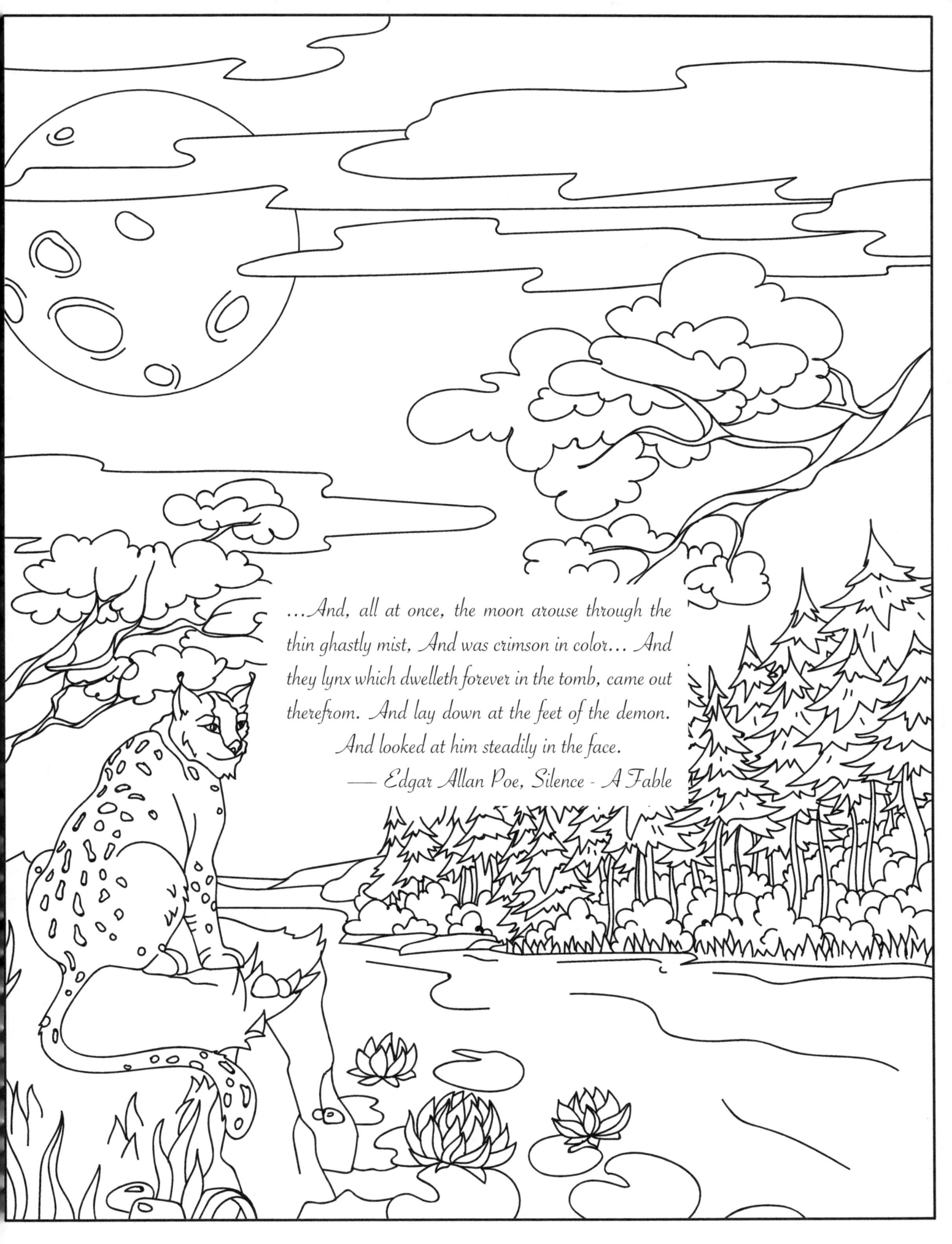

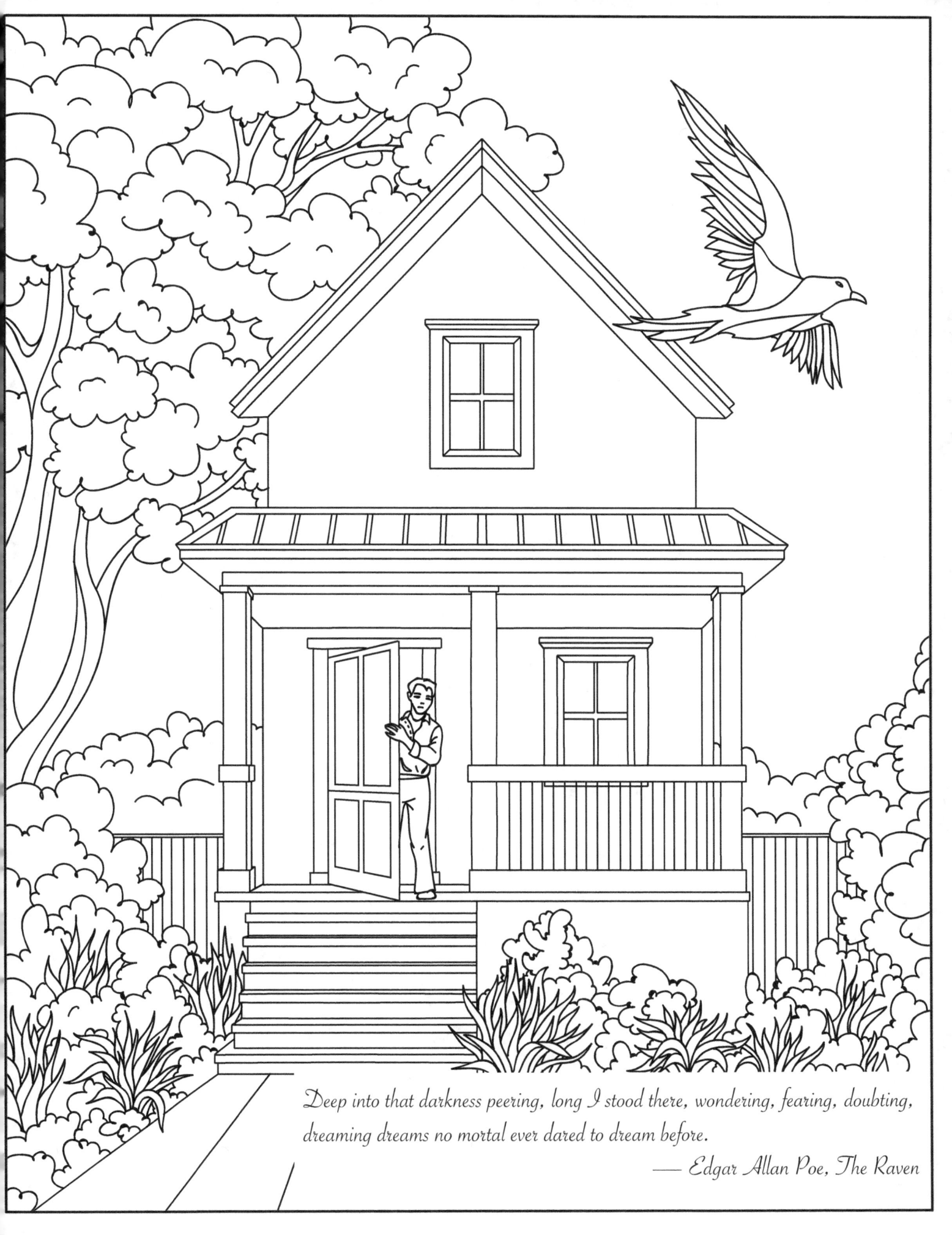

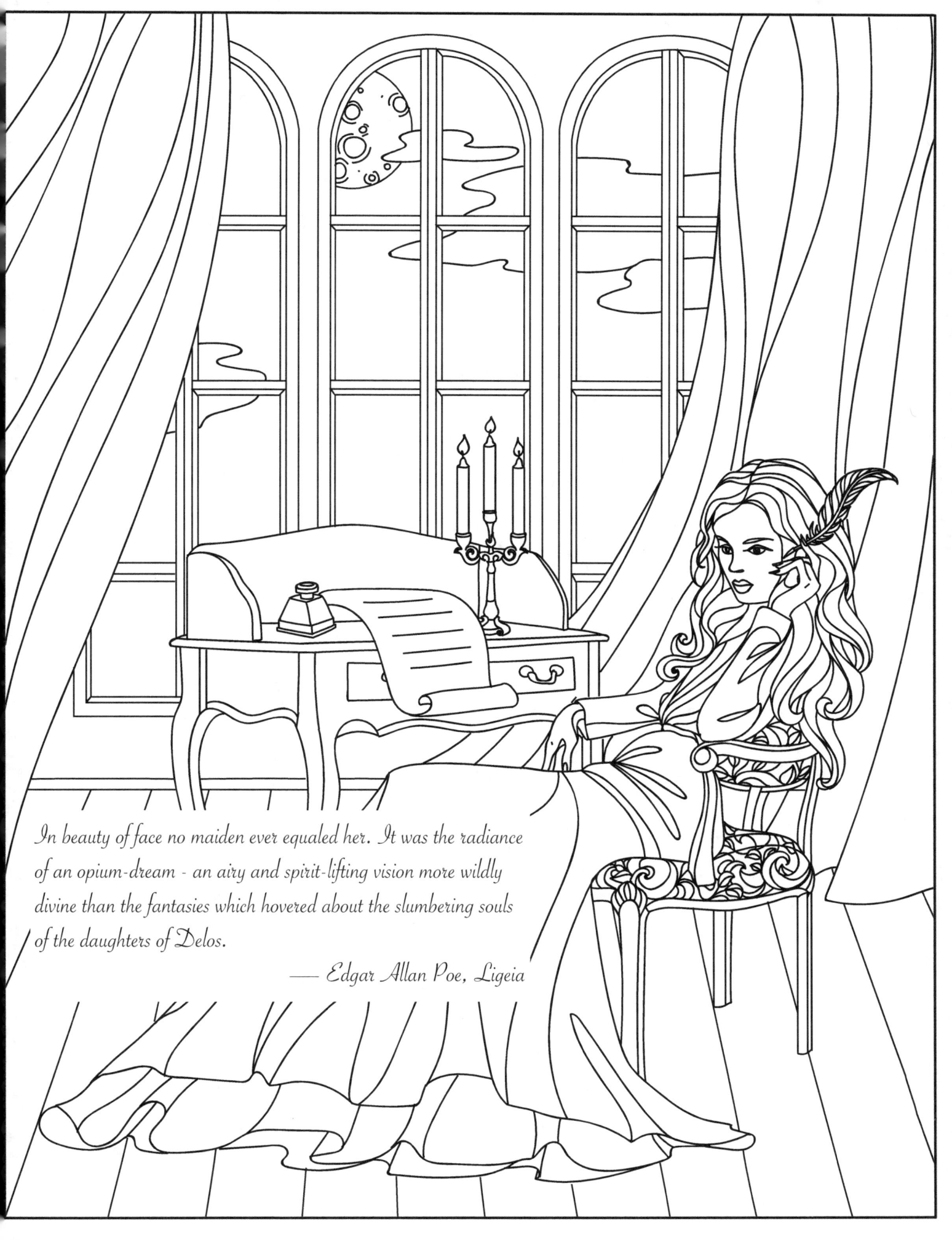

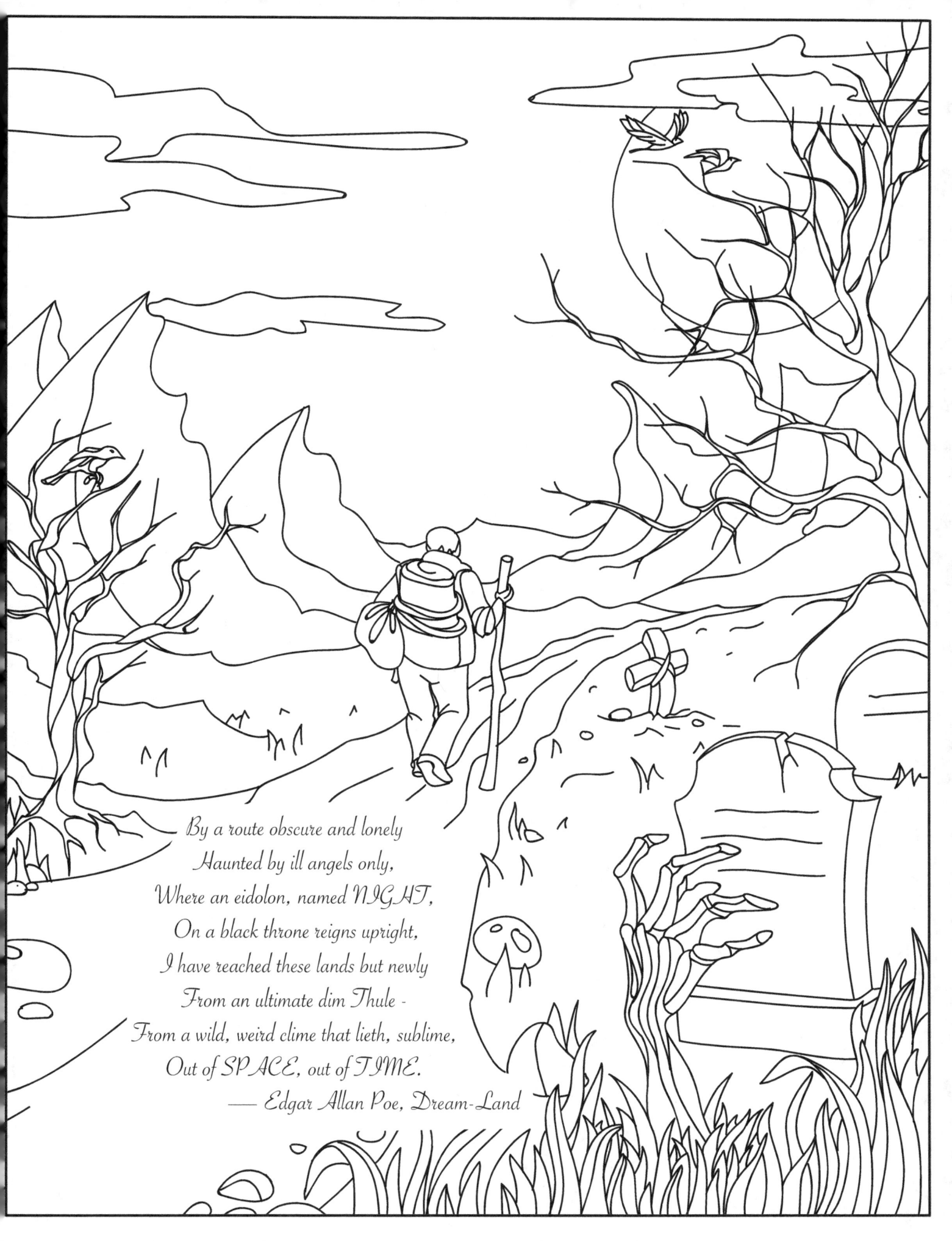

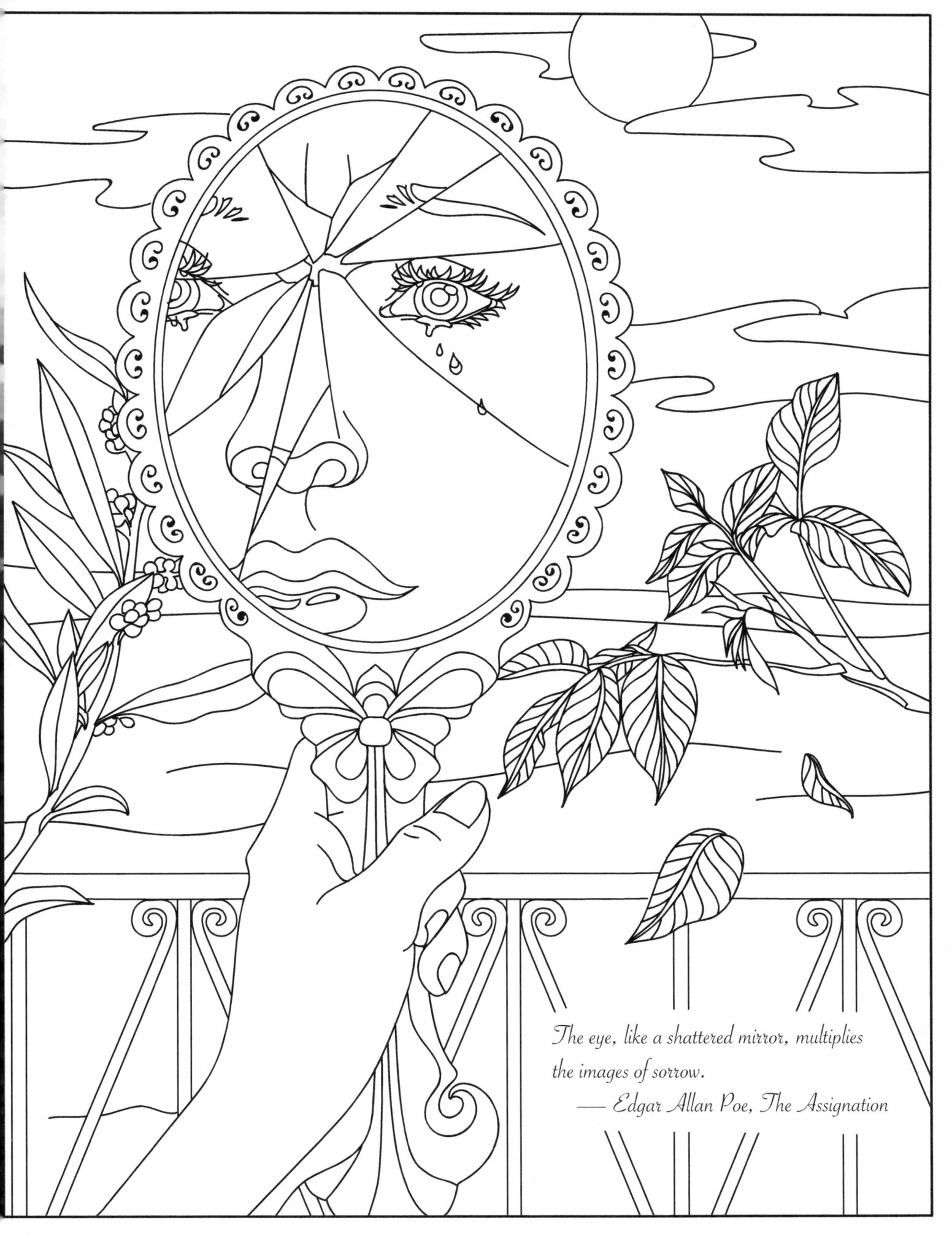

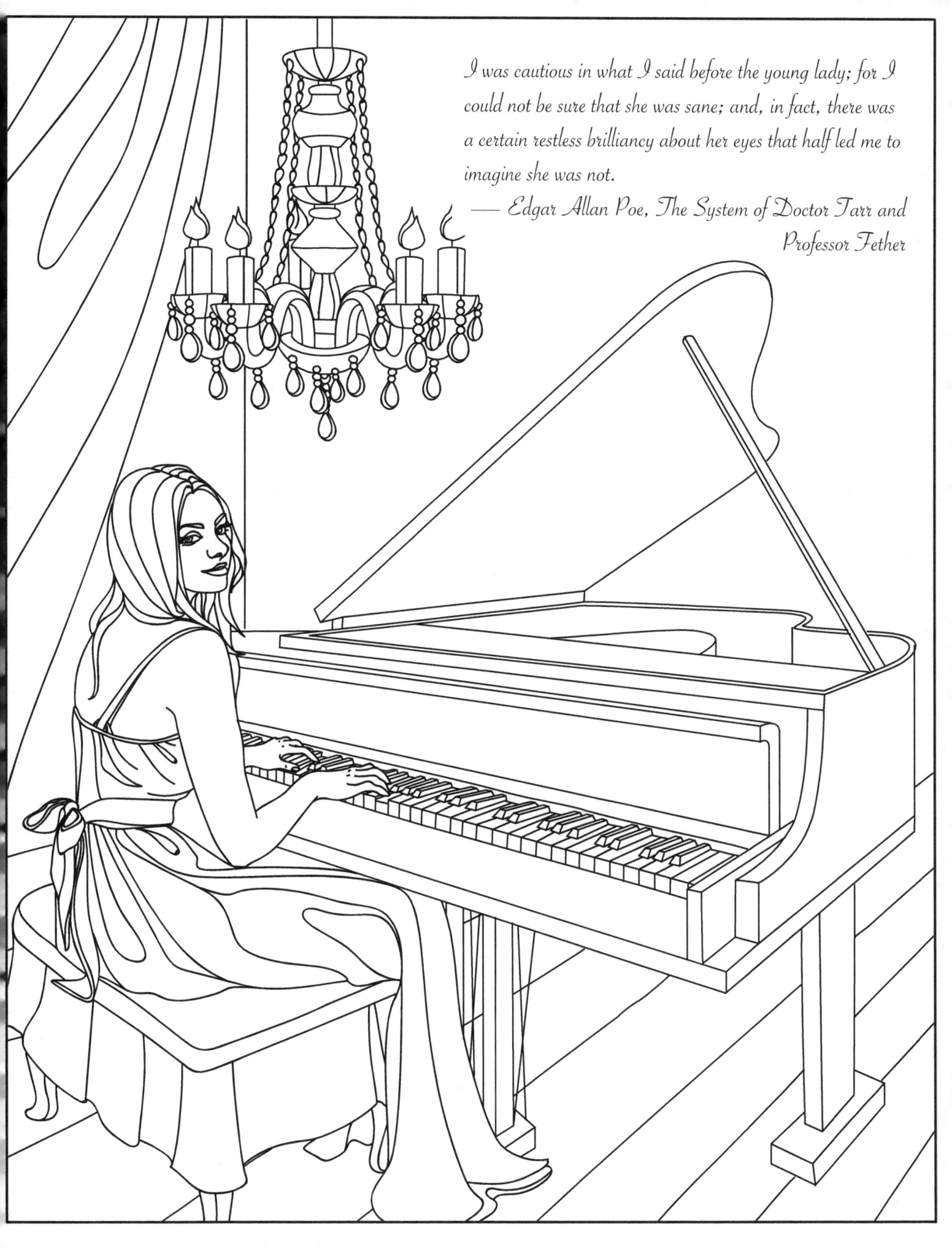

*I was cautious in what I said before the young lady; for I could not be sure that she was sane; and, in fact, there was a certain restless brilliancy about her eyes that half led me to imagine she was not.*
— Edgar Allan Poe, The System of Doctor Tarr and Professor Fether

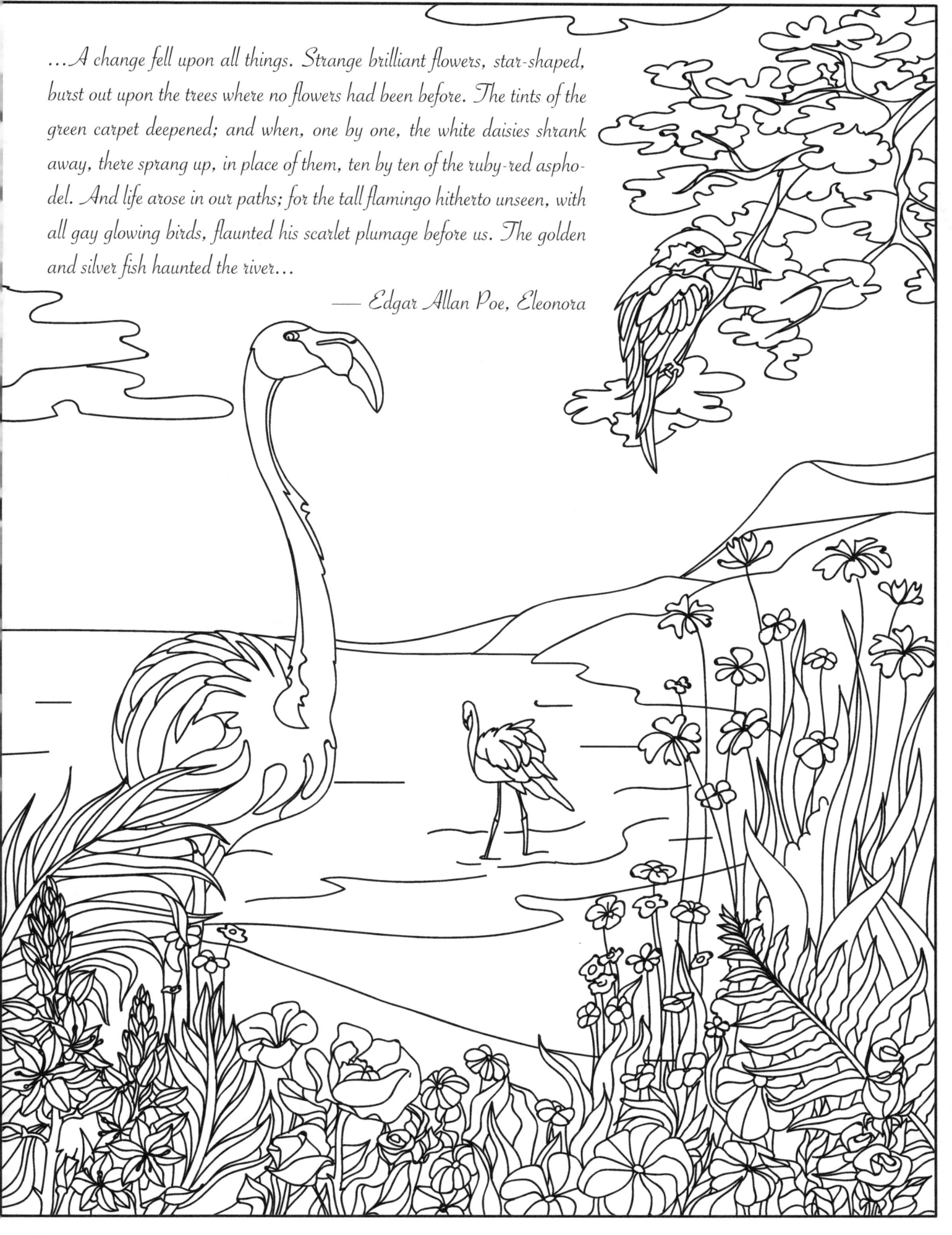

...*A change fell upon all things. Strange brilliant flowers, star-shaped, burst out upon the trees where no flowers had been before. The tints of the green carpet deepened; and when, one by one, the white daisies shrank away, there sprang up, in place of them, ten by ten of the ruby-red asphodel. And life arose in our paths; for the tall flamingo hitherto unseen, with all gay glowing birds, flaunted his scarlet plumage before us. The golden and silver fish haunted the river...*

— Edgar Allan Poe, Eleonora

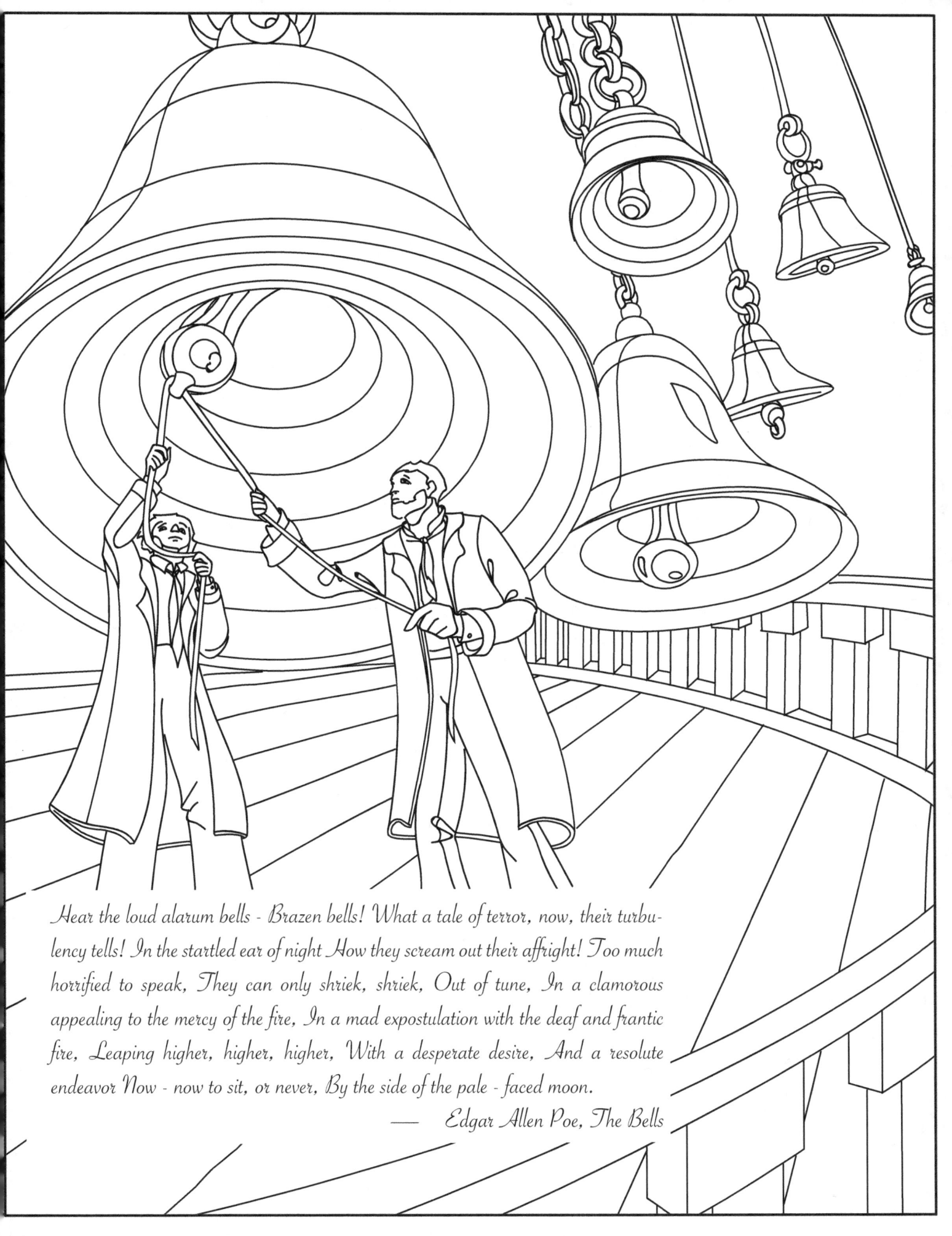

Hear the loud alarum bells - Brazen bells! What a tale of terror, now, their turbulency tells! In the startled ear of night How they scream out their affright! Too much horrified to speak, They can only shriek, shriek, Out of tune, In a clamorous appealing to the mercy of the fire, In a mad expostulation with the deaf and frantic fire, Leaping higher, higher, higher, With a desperate desire, And a resolute endeavor Now - now to sit, or never, By the side of the pale - faced moon.
— Edgar Allen Poe, The Bells

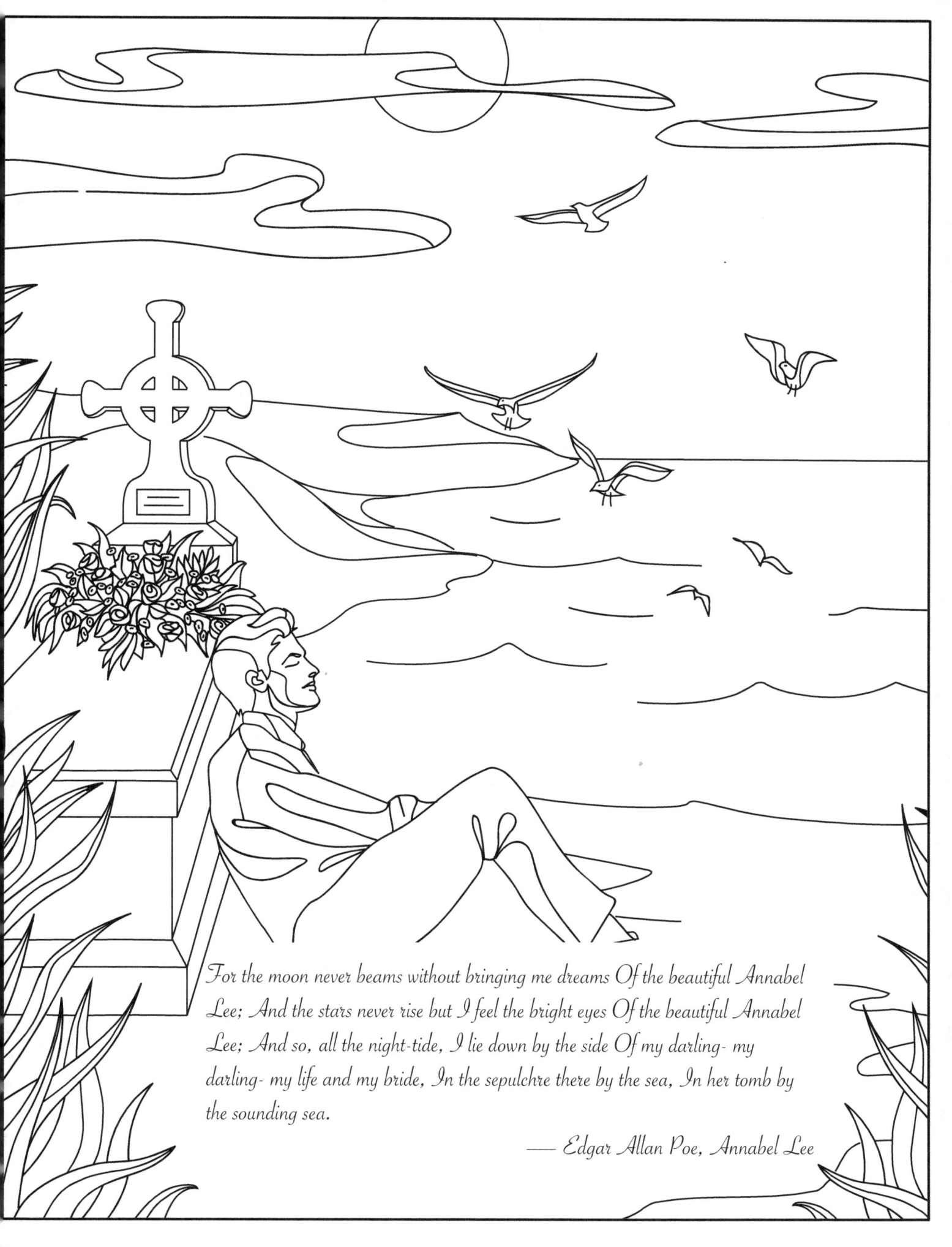

*For the moon never beams without bringing me dreams Of the beautiful Annabel Lee; And the stars never rise but I feel the bright eyes Of the beautiful Annabel Lee; And so, all the night-tide, I lie down by the side Of my darling- my darling- my life and my bride, In the sepulchre there by the sea, In her tomb by the sounding sea.*

— *Edgar Allan Poe, Annabel Lee*

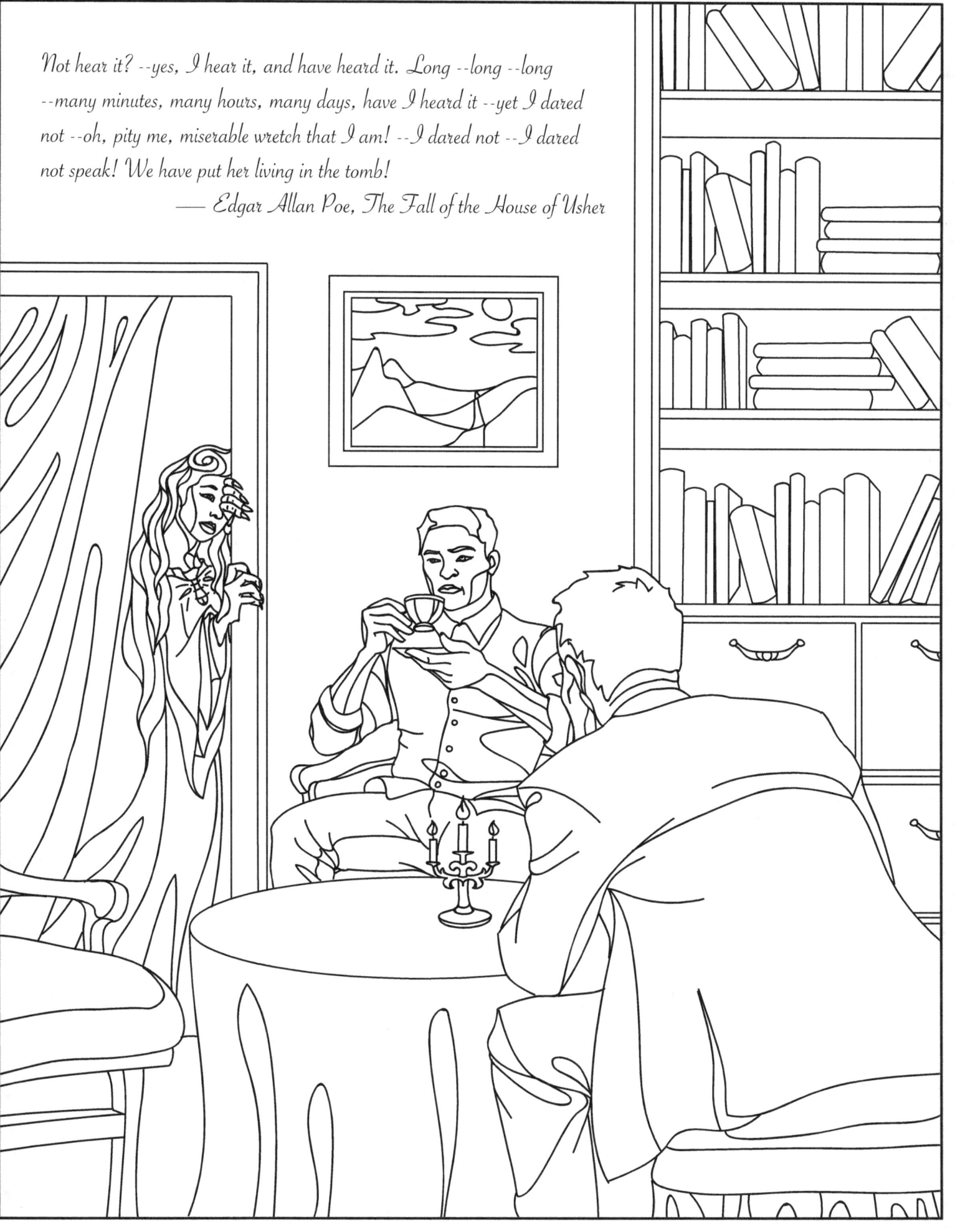

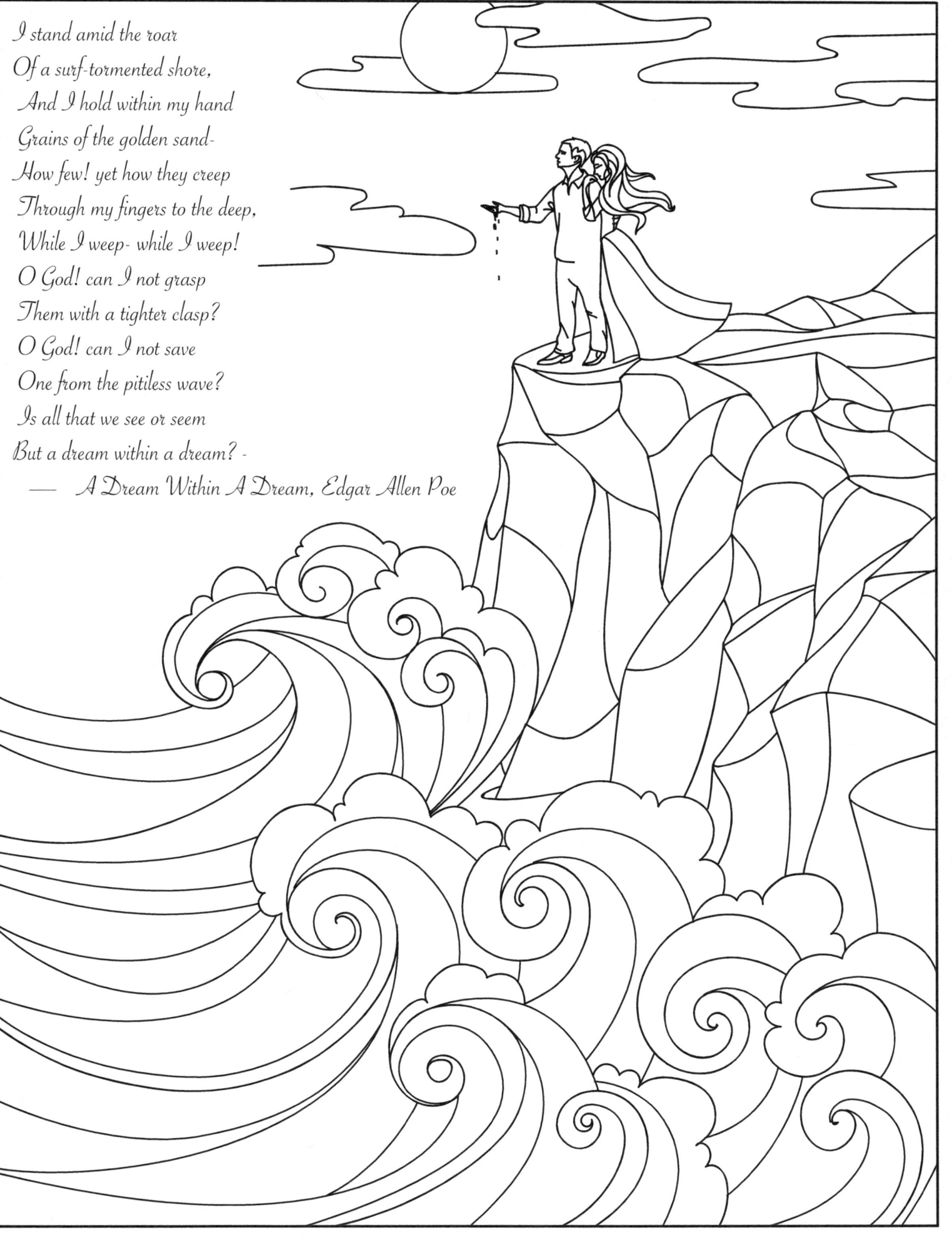

I stand amid the roar
Of a surf-tormented shore,
And I hold within my hand
Grains of the golden sand-
How few! yet how they creep
Through my fingers to the deep,
While I weep- while I weep!
O God! can I not grasp
Them with a tighter clasp?
O God! can I not save
One from the pitiless wave?
Is all that we see or seem
But a dream within a dream? -
— A Dream Within A Dream, Edgar Allen Poe

*The fury of a demon instantly possessed me. I knew myself no longer. My original soul seemed, at once, to take its flight from my body; and a more than fiendish malevolence, gin-nurtured, thrilled every fibre of my frame.*
— Edgar Allan Poe, The Black Cat

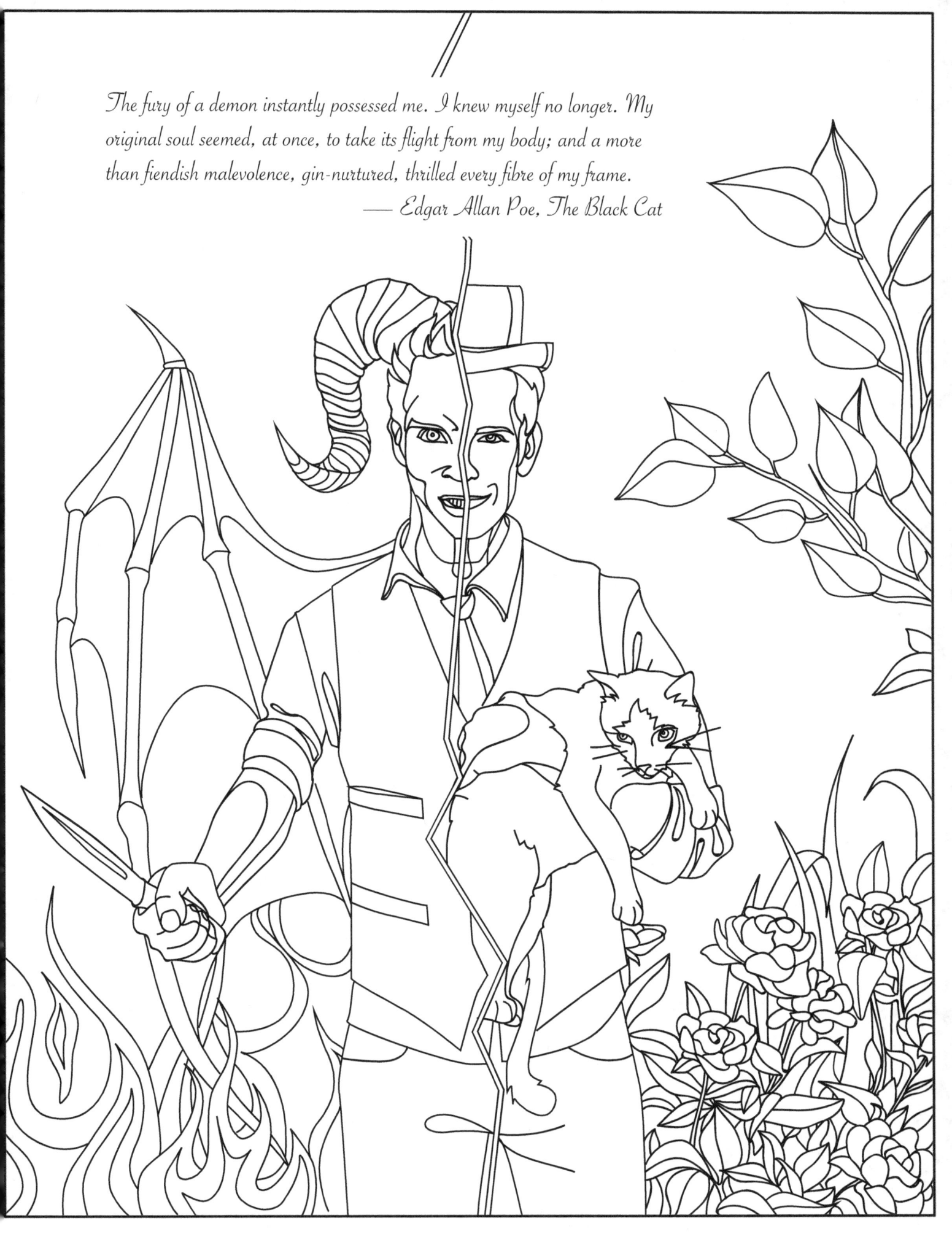

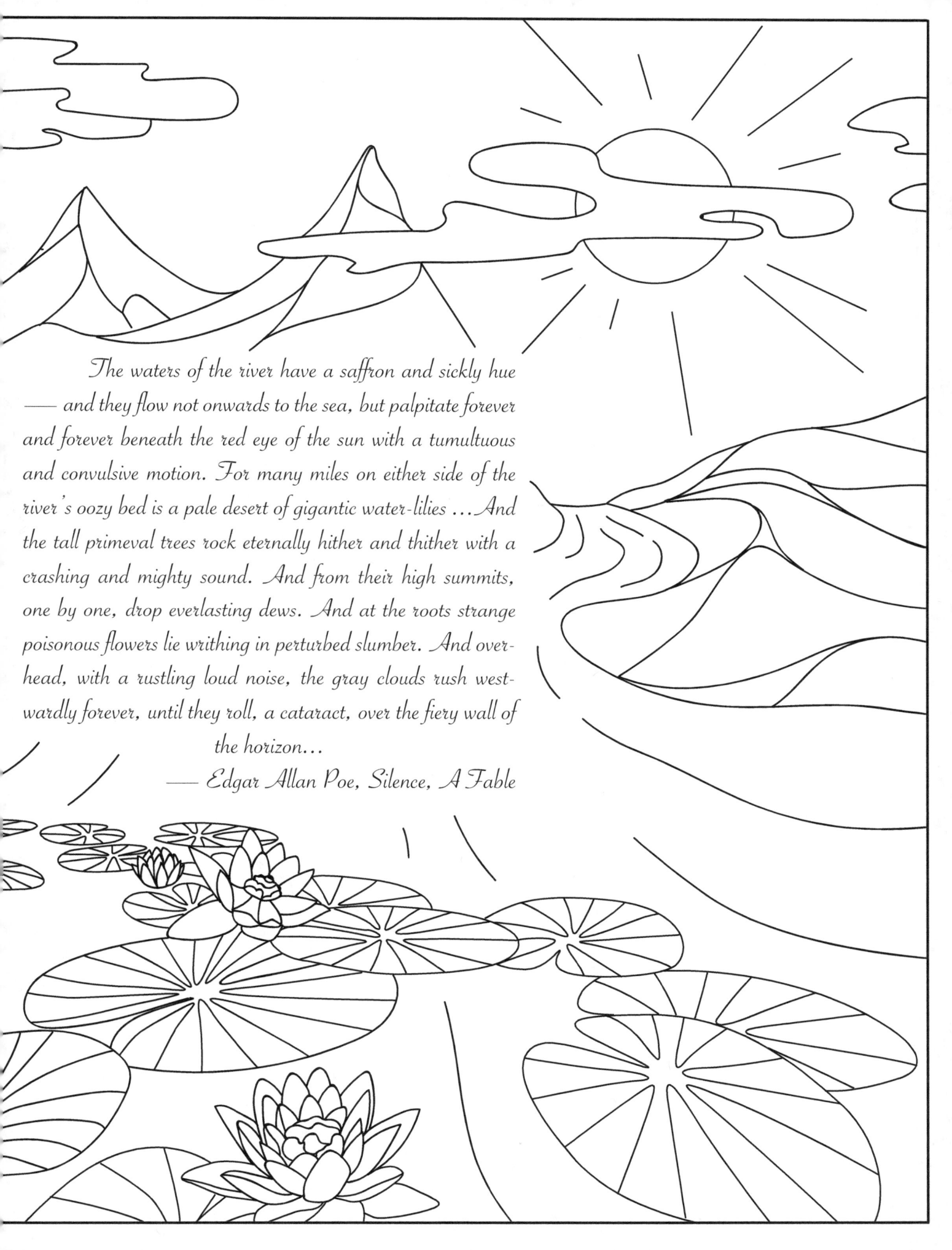

*The waters of the river have a saffron and sickly hue — and they flow not onwards to the sea, but palpitate forever and forever beneath the red eye of the sun with a tumultuous and convulsive motion. For many miles on either side of the river's oozy bed is a pale desert of gigantic water-lilies …And the tall primeval trees rock eternally hither and thither with a crashing and mighty sound. And from their high summits, one by one, drop everlasting dews. And at the roots strange poisonous flowers lie writhing in perturbed slumber. And overhead, with a rustling loud noise, the gray clouds rush westwardly forever, until they roll, a cataract, over the fiery wall of the horizon…*
— *Edgar Allan Poe, Silence, A Fable*

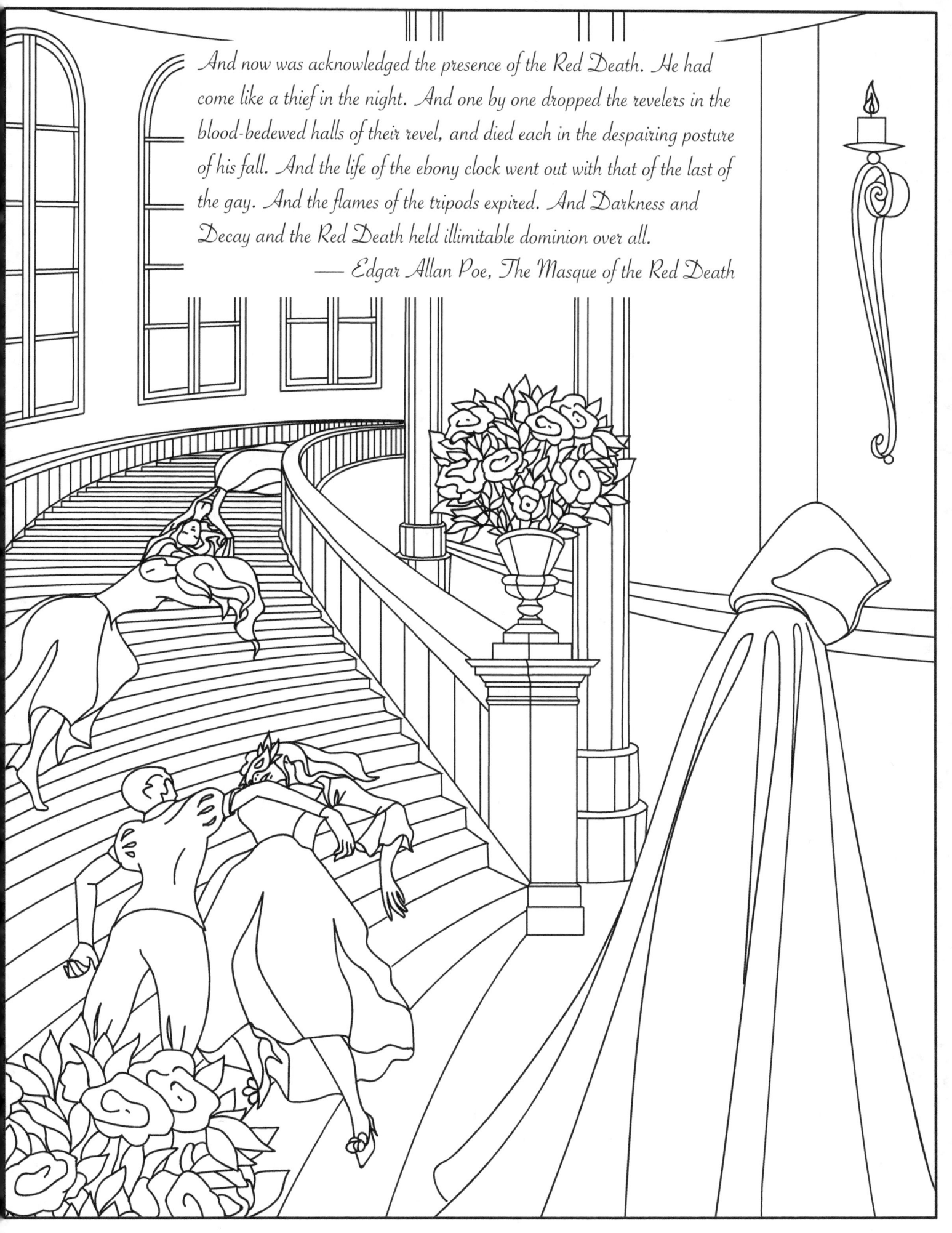

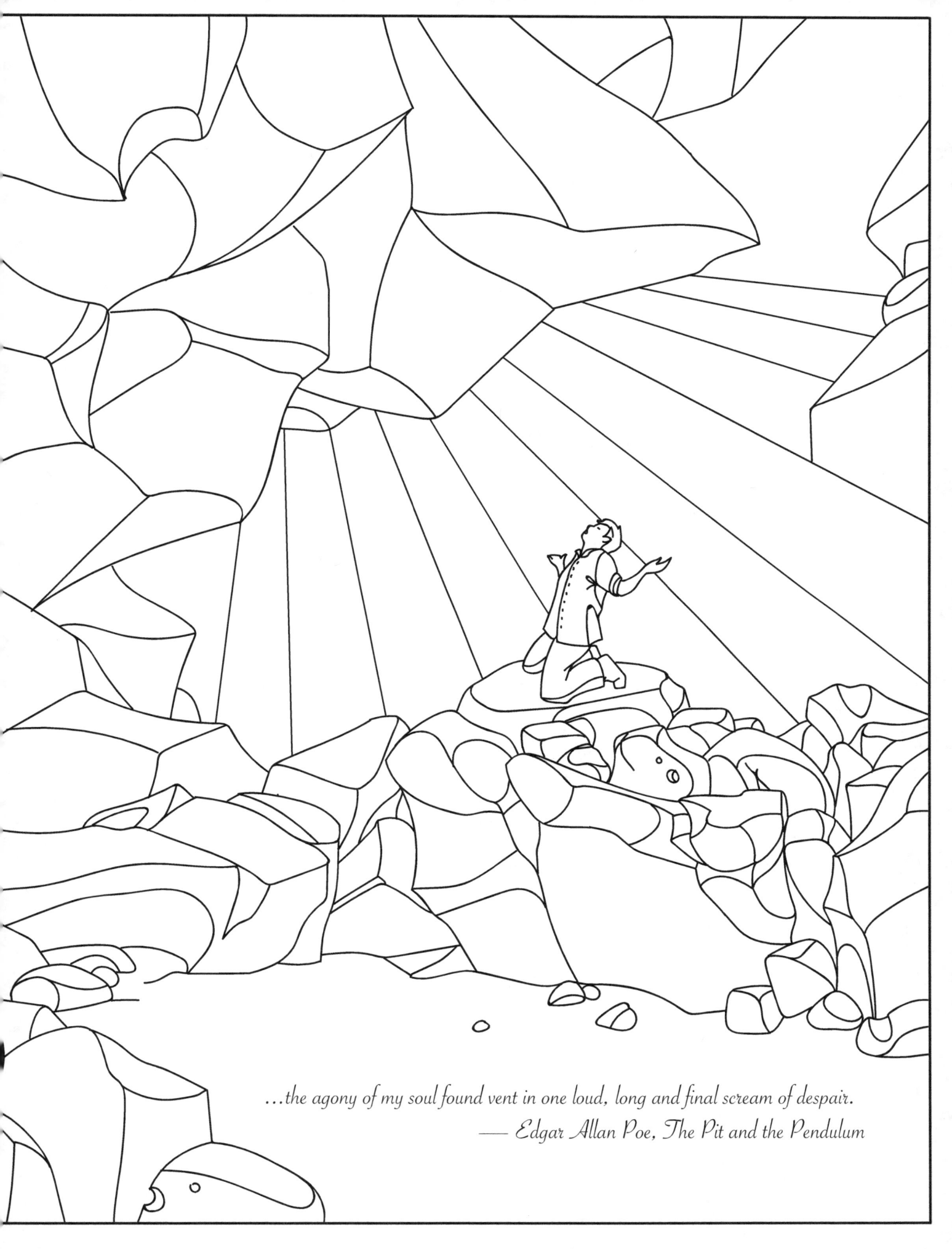

...the agony of my soul found vent in one loud, long and final scream of despair.
— Edgar Allan Poe, The Pit and the Pendulum

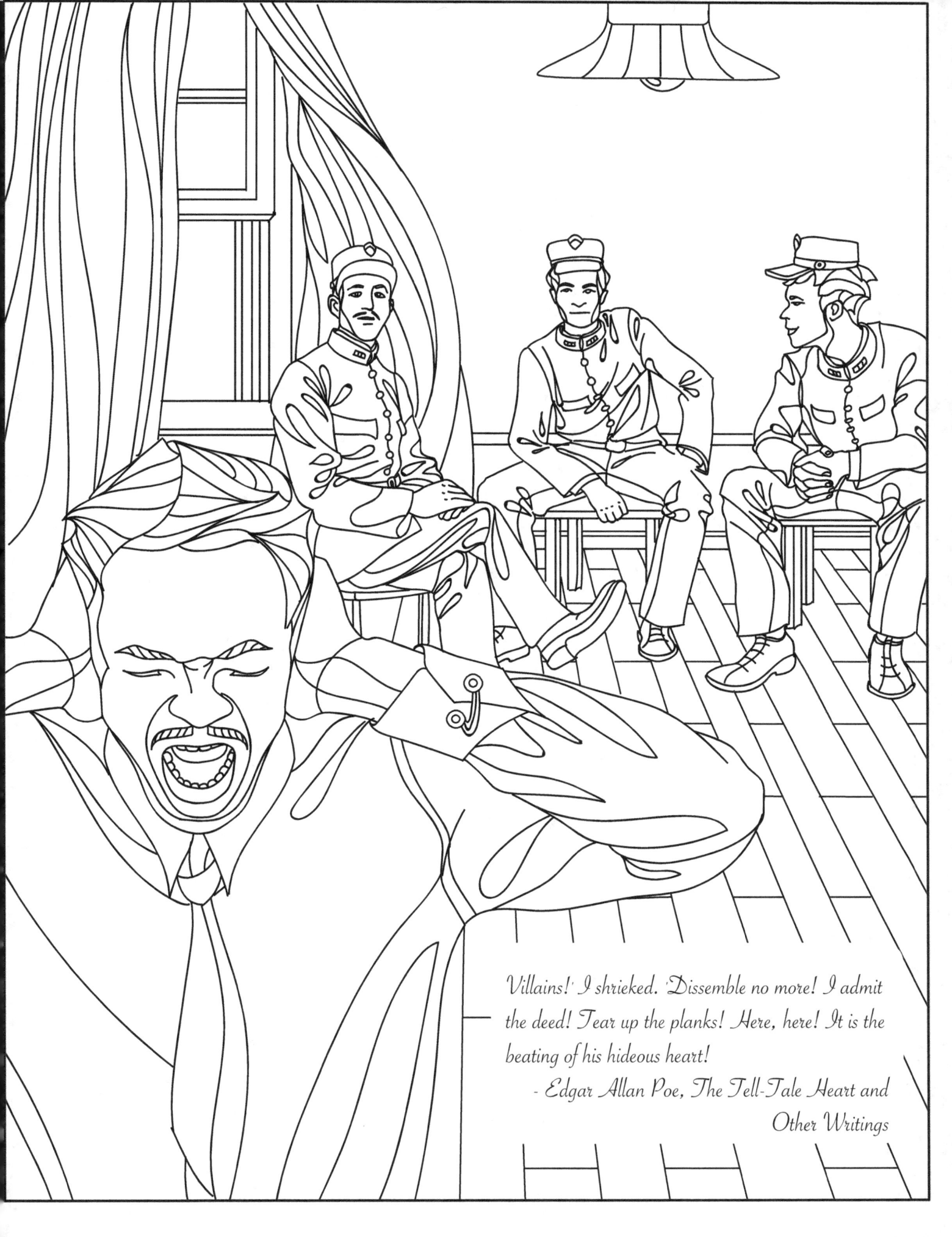

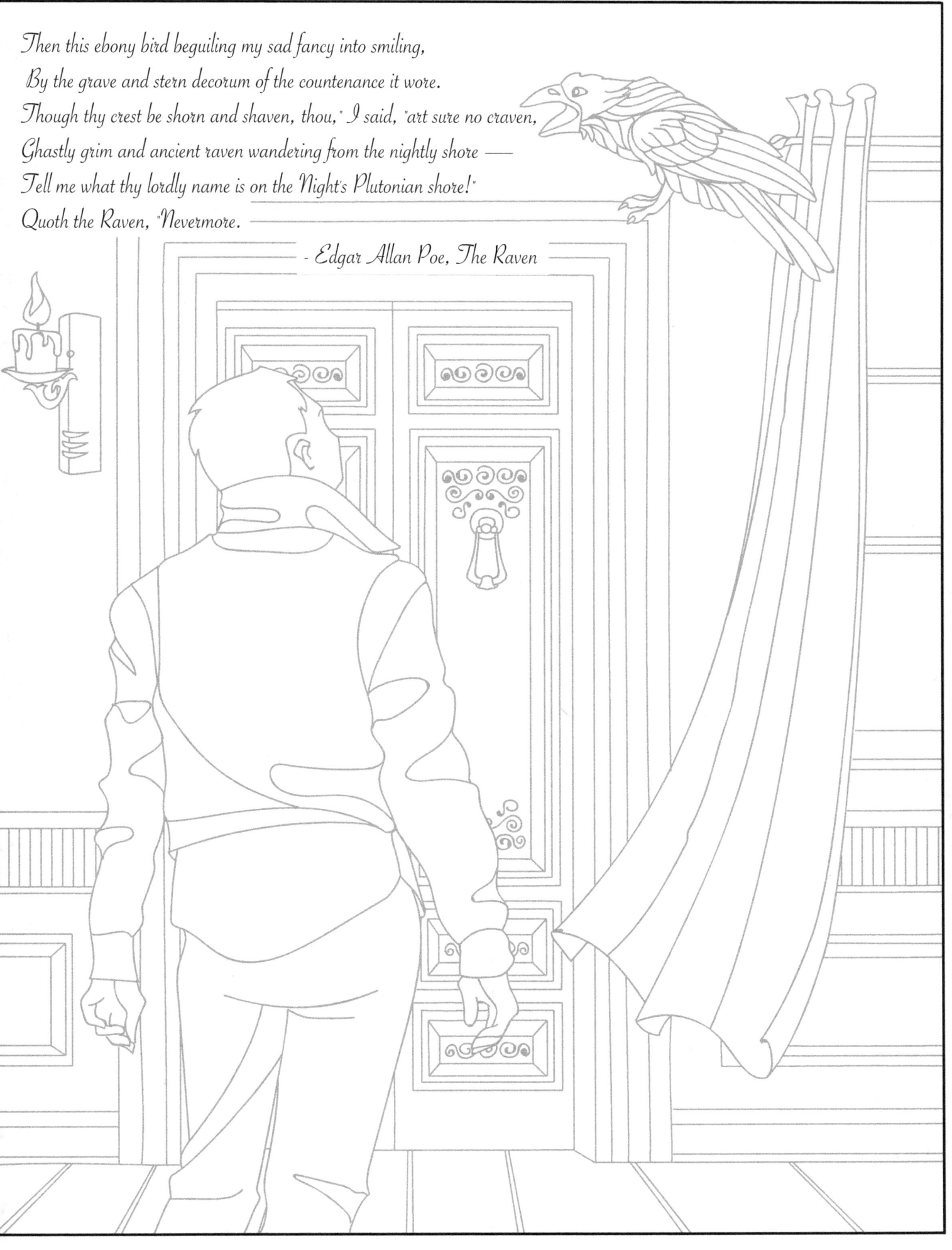

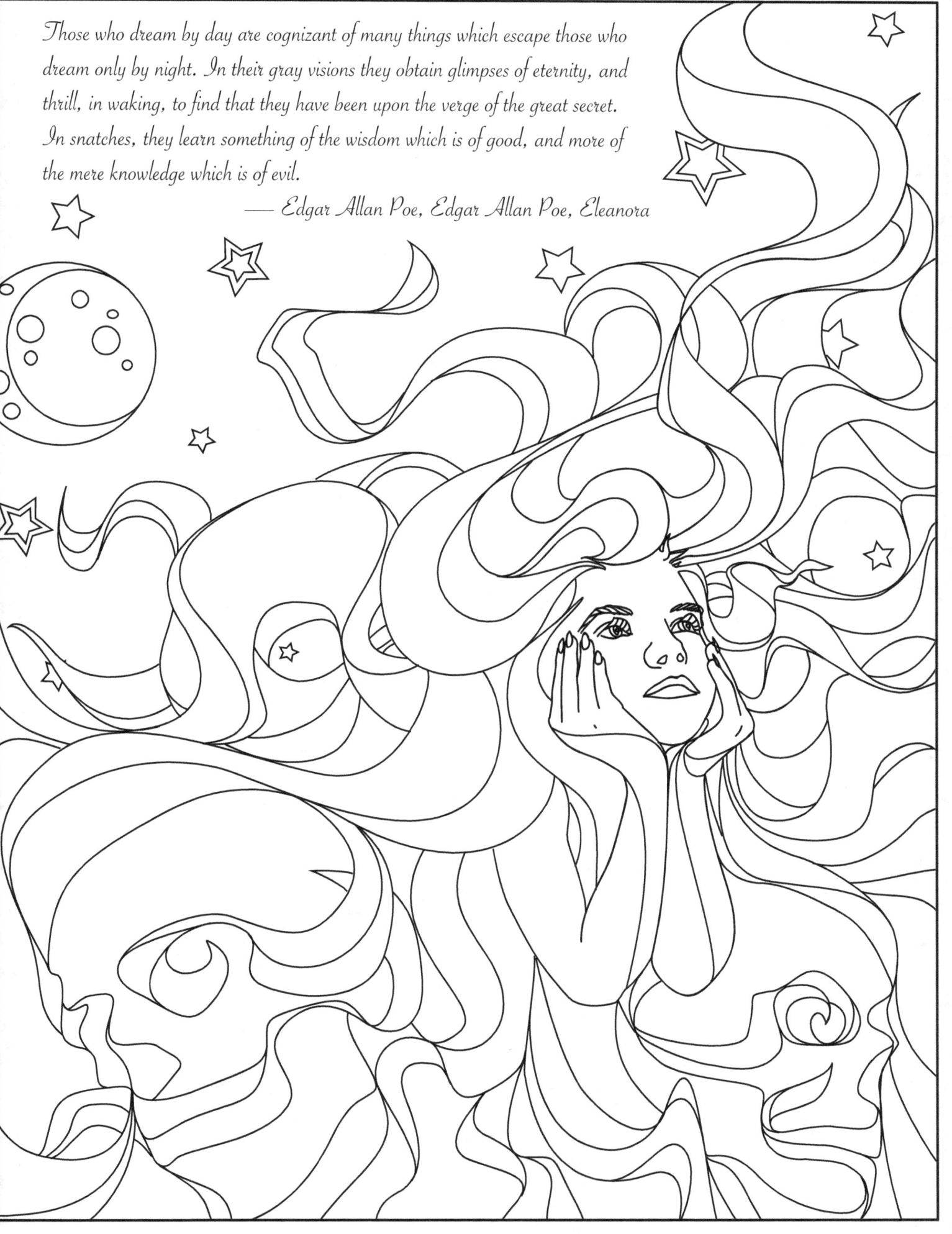

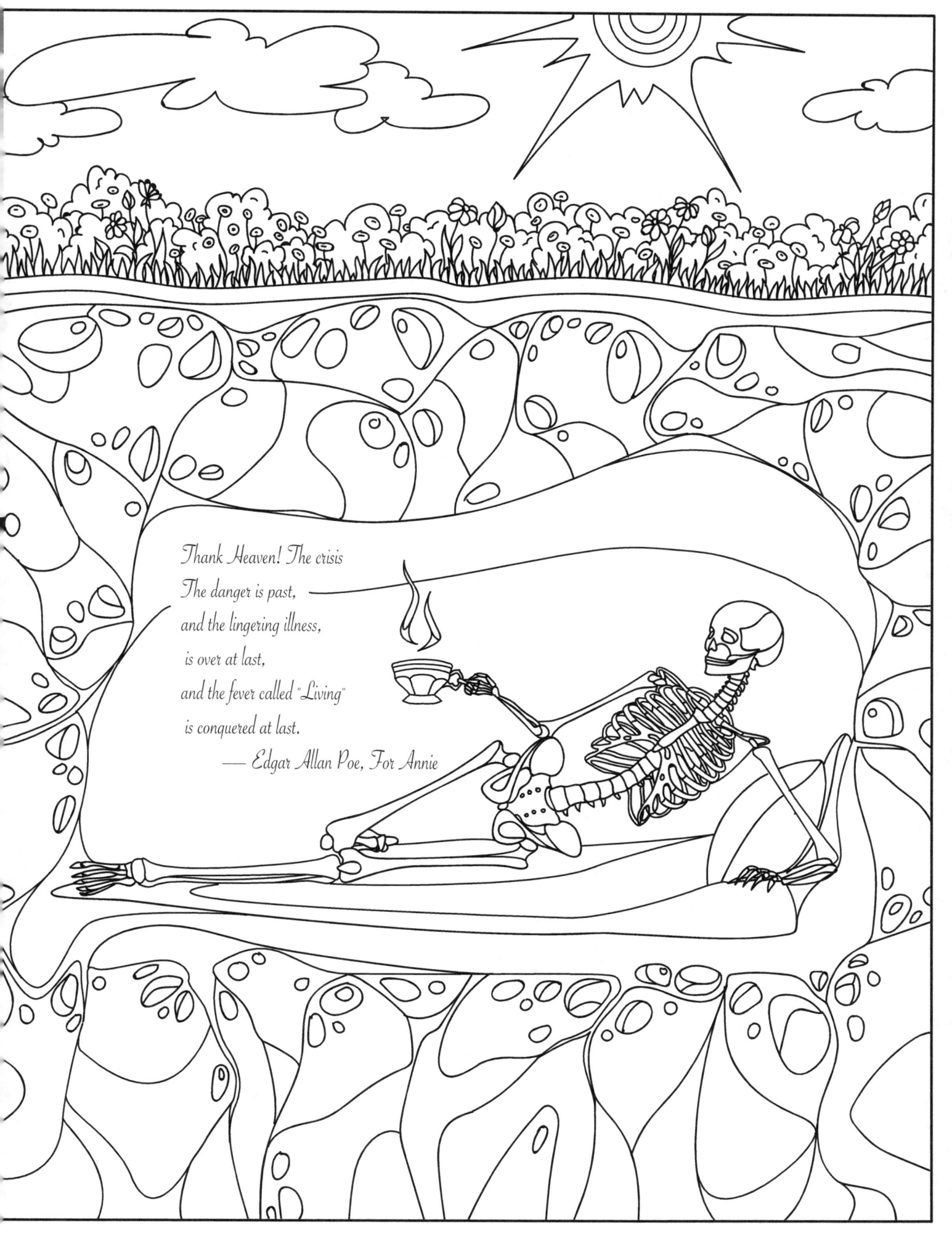

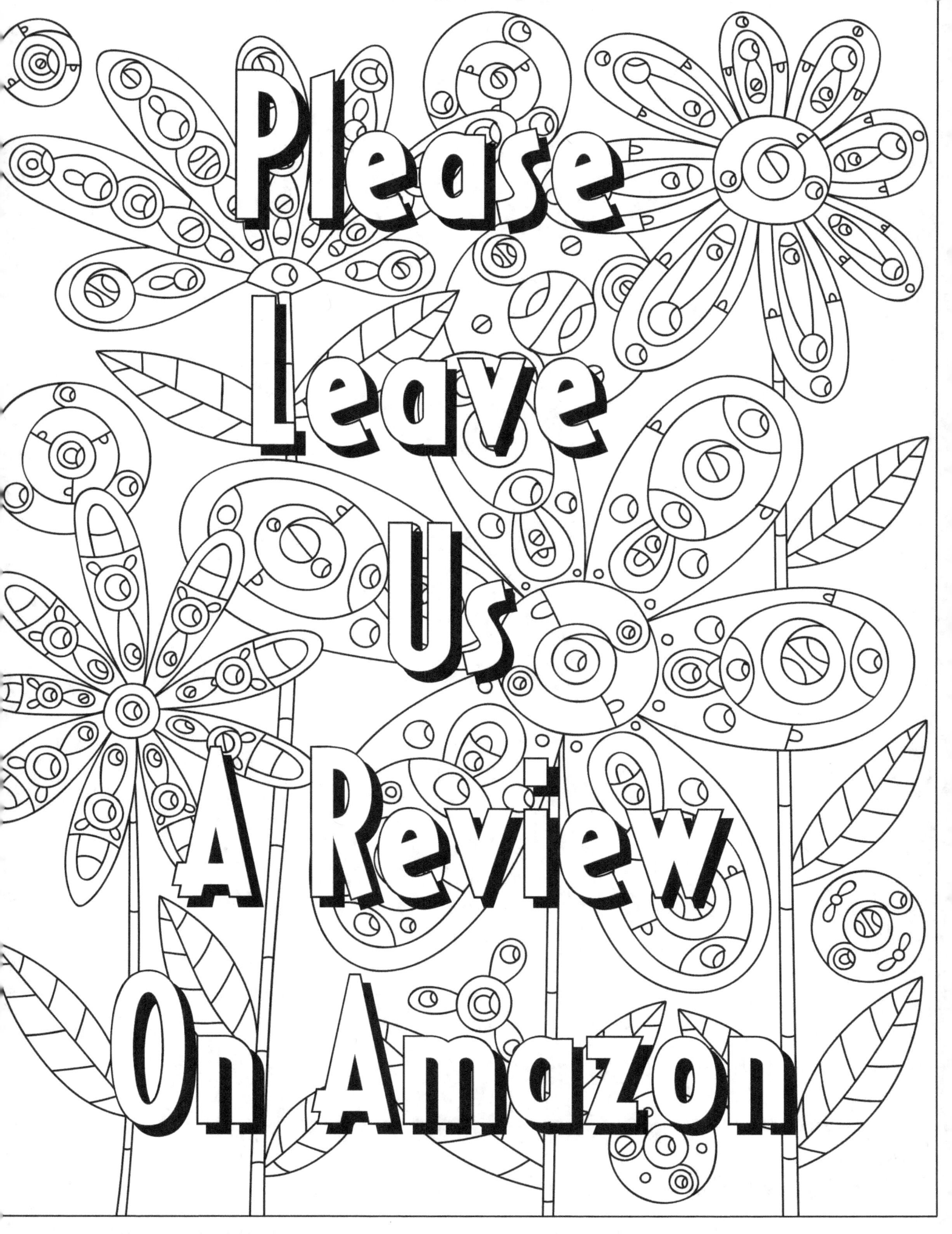